François Ozon

Manchester University Press

FRENCH FILM DIRECTORS

DIANA HOLMES and ROBERT INGRAM *series editors*
DUDLEY ANDREW *series consultant*

FRENCH FILM DIRECTORS

François Ozon

ANDREW ASIBONG

Manchester University Press
MANCHESTER AND NEW YORK

distributed exclusively in the USA by Palgrave

Published by Manchester University Press
Oxford Road, Manchester M13 9NR, UK
and Room 400, 175 Fifth Avenue, New York, NY 10010, USA
www.manchesteruniversitypress.co.uk

Distributed exclusively in the USA by
Palgrave, 175 Fifth Avenue, New York, NY 10010, USA

Distributed exclusively in Canada by
UBC Press, University of British Columbia, 2029 West Mall, Vancouver, BC, Canada V6T 1Z2

British Library Cataloguing-in-Publication Data
A catalogue record for this book is available from the British Library

Library of Congress Cataloging-in-Publication Data applied for

ISBN 978 0 7190 7423 3 *hardback*

First published 2008

17 16 15 14 13 12 11 10 09 08   10 9 8 7 6 5 4 3 2 1

Typeset in Scala with Meta display
by Koinonia, Manchester
Printed in Great Britain
by Biddles Ltd, King's Lynn

Contents

List of plates

Plates 1 and 4 are reproduced by kind permission of Fidélité Films. All other images are reproduced by permission of Jean-Claude Moireau.

Series editors' foreword

To an anglophone audience, the combination of the words 'French' and 'cinema' evokes a particular kind of film: elegant and wordy, sexy but serious – an image as dependent on national stereotypes as is that of the crudely commercial Hollywood blockbuster, which is not to say that either image is without foundation. Over the past two decades, this generalised sense of a significant relationship between French identity and film has been explored in scholarly books and articles, and has entered the curriculum at university level and, in Britain, at A-level. The study of film as an art-form and (to a lesser extent) as industry, has become a popular and widespread element of French Studies, and French cinema has acquired an important place within Film Studies. Meanwhile, the growth in multi-screen and 'art-house' cinemas, together with the development of the video industry, has led to the greater availability of foreign-language films to an English-speaking audience. Responding to these developments, this series is designed for students and teachers seeking information and accessible but rigorous critical study of French cinema, and for the enthusiastic filmgoer who wants to know more.

The adoption of a director-based approach raises questions about auteurism. A series that categorises films not according to period or to genre (for example), but to the person who directed them, runs the risk of espousing a romantic view of film as the product of solitary inspiration. On this model, the critic's role might seem to be that of discovering continuities, revealing a necessarily coherent set of themes and motifs which correspond to the particular genius of the individual. This is not our aim: the auteur perspective on film, itself most clearly articulated in France in the early 1950s, will be interrogated in certain volumes of the series, and, throughout, the director will be treated as one highly significant element in a complex process of film production and reception which includes socio-economic and political determinants, the work of a large and highly skilled team of artists and technicians, the mechanisms of production and distribution, and the complex and multiply determined responses of spectators.

The work of some of the directors in the series is already known outside France, that of others is less so – the aim is both to provide informative and original English-language studies of established figures, and to extend the range of French directors known to anglophone students of cinema. We intend the series to contribute to the promotion of the informal and formal study of French films, and to the pleasure of those who watch them.

DIANA HOLMES
ROBERT INGRAM

Acknowledgements

I would like to thank Emma Wilson and Lisa Downing for their practical encouragement at the time I was trying to get my book proposal off the ground, as well as the series editors Diana Holmes and Robert Ingram for accepting it. The guidance of Patrick ffrench (in the book's early stages), Peter Hallward (before the book was even thought of) and Helen Vassallo (in its final stages) has been invaluable. I am grateful to Alison Macdonald and Scott Smith for reading the whole book as soon as the first draft was written, and for being such thoughtful and inspiring interlocutors over Ozon matters. For other specific moments of research-related support, thanks also to: Emma Campbell, Michelle Chilcoat, Thomas Deltombe, Hannah Eaton, Fiona Handyside, Jacob Harders, Corinne Ranaraja, Daniel Rosen and Lisa Walsh. I am indebted to Frances Christodoulou, Christy Constantakopoulou and Peter Liddel for acts of generosity, without which I may not have completed the book. Huge thanks are due to Sonia El-Amine, Céline Farchi, Sandrine Fauvin, Manu, Henri Pauly and Bertrand Peyri for putting me up so hospitably during recent research trips to France and Belgium. I am grateful to Charlotte Maignan at Fidélité Films, Jean-Claude Moireau and François Ozon for their help in providing the book's images. Finally, I want to thank all my students and colleagues at Birkbeck, University of London, for providing such a wonderful atmosphere in which to teach and research, and especially Michael Temple for his advice and Akane Kawakami for sharing our office so selflessly. This book is for Scott Smith.

Family filmmaker: an introduction to François Ozon

If one thing can be said with certainty about François Ozon's career in filmmaking, it is this: it has moved with a lightning rapidity. The fact that between the ages of 30 and 40 – from 1997 to 2007 – he wrote and directed no fewer than nine feature films, all of which gained international distribution, widespread controversy (often accompanied by prizes and great acclaim), and not inconsiderable amounts of money (his 2001 film *8 femmes* has made over $3 million dollars to date at the American box office alone) is not merely anecdotal.[1] It is not enough simply to proceed from a statement of these facts towards a platitudinous enunciation of Ozon's often-repeated status as 'boy wonder' or *enfant terrible* of turn-of-the-millennium French cinema: we ought, perhaps, to linger on the significance of this speed. Ozon's films ceaselessly revolve around the question of dynamic movement, shift, progress and change; his characters are often propelled by forces whose capacity to catapult individuals into other dimensions is quite otherworldly in its charge, stealth and intensity.

Like the eponymous heroine of his 2006 melodrama *Angel*, François Ozon appeared to be anticipating the success of his adult

---

1 Some prizes Ozon's films have won include: Valladolid International Film Festival: Silver Spike (*Le Temps qui reste*, 2005); Bangkok World Film Festival: Best Film (*Swimming Pool*, 2003); Berlin International Film Festival: Reader Jury of the 'Berliner Morgenpost' (*8 femmes*, 2002); New York Lesbian and Gay Film Festival: Best Feature (*Gouttes d'eau sur pierres brûlantes*, 2000); L.A. Outfest: Grand Jury, Outstanding Foreign Narrative Feature (*Les Amants criminels*, 2000); Avignon Film Festival: Prix Panavision (*Scènes de lit*, 1998); Brest European Short Film Festival: French Grand Prix (*Une Robe d'été*, 1996); French Syndicate of Cinema Critics: Critics Award, Best Short (*Action vérité*, 1996).

creations from an early age. Still a schoolboy, Ozon, inspired by his father's Super-8 projections of the Ozon family and of trips to India, had already started making short films. Between the ages of 18 and 22 he had made over thirty Super-8 productions of his own, famously railroading his teacher parents and his three younger siblings into appearing in these often rather shocking and revelatory pieces. Even a cursory glance at some of these juvenilia, makes clear the sheer precocity of Ozon's cinematic vision, confirming just how keen the young Ozon was to generate concrete images for his peculiarly family-orientated preoccupations. In the 7-minute, silent *Photo de famille* (1988) the twenty-one-year-old Ozon casts both his parents, together with his brother Guillaume and sister Julie, in a macabre little farce about death and its eruption into family life that contains, in seedling, all the themes that would flower in feature films such as *Sitcom* (1998) and *8 femmes* (2001), as well as in early professional shorts such as *Victor* (1993) and *La Petite Mort* (1994). An adult son cheerfully murders his family one evening (he stabs his sister, poisons his mother, and suffocates his father). The dirty act done, he arranges the three cadavers respectably and upright on the family sofa, takes his place among them, and poses for the camera he has set up on the table. The film is pure Ozon in its fusion of absurd comedy and horror. Mixed in with this grotesquerie, as will always be the case even in Ozon's most seemingly inconsequential work, is a central – and weighty – underlying concept: the adult son's subjec- tivity is dependent on the simultaneous destruction of the family *and* its preservation in artificial, frozen form, a form that lies totally under his control. Ozon shows us a protagonist haunted by his family, caught in the deadlock of wanting them out of the way (for reasons unspecified) and yet being compelled to arrange himself in accor- dance with their positioning, dead or alive. With *Photo de famille*, the young filmmaker Ozon manipulates and 'kills' his own (amusingly complicit) family in the creation of a violently personal piece of art: as he has often jokily remarked, it was clearly preferable that he should kill them on film than for real. In the 12-minute, silent *Mes parents un jour d'été* (1990), Ozon traps his parents René and Anne-Marie even more sadistically in their role as actors before the camera's gaze. The father in particular is eroticised and laid bare in a way that makes him oddly reminiscent of the naked forest ogre in Ozon's queer fairy tale of 1998, *Les Amants criminels*. Once more, then, the film anticipates the themes and aesthetics of many later Ozon films, especially in its evocation of the inherent isolation within the couple relation. Ozon shoots his parents in a number of summer holiday afternoon situations: Papa rides his bicycle alone, while Maman goes shopping in the village alone. Cross-cutting between the two solitary activities Ozon highlights the simultaneity of utterly separate pursuits. When the couple are together within the same scene they appear to squabble ceaselessly, and every activity (even Scrabble) seems to throw up obstacles to harmony. At one point, out walking together in the mountains, Maman seems tempted to push Papa to his death. The film's final image, of the pair reconciled at the village graveyard, contains a whiff of the (perhaps already ironically) optimistic belief in the possibility of unified relations via an exposure to ritualised death that we will see in the final frames of *Sitcom* and *8 femmes*.

François Ozon was born in Paris to René and Anne-Marie Ozon on November 15, 1967. This book takes as one of its points of departure the idea that Ozon has consciously styled his œuvre thus far around a number of recurring tropes and themes, one of the most striking of which has been the emergence of adult sexualities and relations (or non-relations) from out of the spectral carcasses of real or fantasised family members. Kinship (impossible or otherwise), desire (frustrated or relentless) and violence (usually lasting beyond the grave) thus structure the narratives of all the films under discussion, and can be seen to stamp Ozon's repertoire of images firmly with the mark of a self-styled *auteur*. Mark Hain (2007: 277), questioning the validity of such a term with reference to Ozon, asks: '[C]an a filmmaker whose work is so disparate in style and tone really be called an *auteur*? And furthermore, does the grandiose and rather nostalgic term carry much meaning for a filmmaker like Ozon?' But although Ozon's films appear sometimes to lurch wildly between tones and registers, often following the pattern of an alternating series of colourful farces and sombre dramas, the *fil rouge* or underlying 'thin red line' of continuity, of which the actress Jeanne Moreau speaks when discussing Ozon's (for her, admirable) consistency as a filmmaker, is clearly discernible as soon as we begin to scratch beneath the surface.

Ozon's cinema employs a number of recurring elements, all of which combine to generate the image of a certain solidity of vision beyond the coherent aesthetic and philosophical currents that will take up so much discussion in this book. Like many film *auteurs*, Ozon has depended on the return in film after film of the same (usually female) faces. Thus we find the Spanish actress Lucía Sánchez in three of the early shorts (*Une Robe d'été*, 1996; *X2000*, 1998; *Scènes de lit*, 1997) and in the key role of the maid Maria in the first feature, *Sitcom*. The French actress, screenwriter and director Marina de Van crops up as the terrifying Tatiana of *Regarde la mer* (1997) and as the dutiful daughter Sophie in *Sitcom*, and has also (along with occasional collaborator Emmanuèle Bernheim) assisted Ozon in the writing of a number of his screenplays. Another young French actress, Ludivine Sagnier, stars in three Ozon features (*Gouttes d'eau sur pierres brûlantes*, 1999; *8 femmes*; *Swimming Pool*, 2003) and provides the voice of Angel in the dubbed French version of the film of the same name. And the English actress Charlotte Rampling has famously had her film career revived by acclaimed appearances in a string of Ozon's twenty-first-century films, *Sous le sable* (2000), *Swimming Pool* (2003) and *Angel* (2006). In addition to the familiar faces that pop up in film after film directed by Ozon, music, movement and costume design have acquired a consistency of tone too. The composer Philippe Rombi has composed the original score for the vast majority of Ozon's features, his usually heavy and brooding pieces conferring an immediate musical individuality upon the films in question. The vibrant Sébastien Charles shimmies his way through his role as the song-loving boyfriend in the early short *Une Robe d'été*, only to re-present his distinctive moves some years later in altered and altogether more grandiose form, this time through his work as the choreographer responsible for the famous dances of the eight actresses of the landmark *8 femmes*. Pascaline Chavanne's costume design has lent different forms of an unfashionably baroque look to films as dissimilar as *5x2* (2004), *Un Lever de rideau* (2006) and *Angel*. This persistence in using the same team or 'tribe' of colourful workers for the fabrication of every brick of his 'film-house' lends Ozon's films an instantly recognisable stamp. Not unlike Spain's Pedro Almodóvar (born 1949), Germany's Rainer Werner Fassbinder (1945–82) and Baltimore's John Waters (born 1946), whose films so often spin around the reassuringly predictable presence of faces fans just *know* will weave in and out of film after film, Ozon's design seems from the outset to have been to engender a whole extended family through his cinema.

Almodóvar, Fassbinder and Waters are clearly important reference points for Ozon quite apart from the example they set as new filmic fathers, patriarchs of a brood of anti-patriarchal sons and (more often) daughters. The profound understanding all three of these filmmakers have demonstrated of the significance of the so-called 'women's picture', fused with their gleeful revelry in the on-screen representation of extreme camp, kitsch and trash, has brought to each of their respective national cinemas a collection of films that routinely assault and violate comfortable modes of viewing, shoving the spectator into an arena of lovingly prepared filth, beauty and artifice. Ozon's early films in particular pay persistent homage to the disgustingly funny and deadly serious possibilities opened up by the holy trinity of 1970s and 1980s cinematic excess. It is difficult to watch *Sitcom*, for example, without getting the feeling that at any moment the maid is going to prepare an Almodovarian gazpacho spiked with barbiturates; *Gouttes d'eau sur pierres brûlantes* took Ozon's clear fondness for Fassbinder's horrific on-screen mental cruelty to the point where he would actually adapt one of the German's plays; and even a film as late as *Angel* is a good deal easier to swallow when one can see the eponymous heroine's overblown smirks and cringe-worthily comical grimaces as the direct descendants of a performance by John Waters divas Mink Stole or Divine. If Ozon's films usually lack the genuine emotional highs and lows often generated by Almodóvar, Fassbinder and Waters, though, this is surely down to the way in which Ozon so confidently repackages their aesthetics within the ironic framework of a devastatingly knowing – and extremely French – cleverness. Even if Ozon's cinema is deeply marked by the raw influence of the Spanish, German and American sons of melodrama, his is ultimately a studiedly intellectual project.

Ozon must be understood as a filmmaker who has formally analysed film – its history, its theory, its practice – and as a *cinéaste* who has, from the start of his career, but most obviously in a film like *8 femmes*, delighted in displaying his brilliant knowledge of cinema. He obtained a Master's degree in cinematographic studies at the University of Paris I (he wrote his dissertation on the film director Maurice Pialat), and subsequently attended the prestigious French film school FEMIS (from where he graduated in 1993), studying under the tutelage of both the film director Eric Rohmer and the *Cahiers du cinéma* critic/filmmaker/actor Jean Douchet. One can catch a glimpse of the pre-famous Ozon among a group of FEMIS student directors interviewed for a British television documentary in 1992 about the French 'New Wave' of the late 1950s and early 1960s. In the programme, he upbraids a fellow-student for the latter's misunderstanding of Claude Chabrol, demonstrating not only his enthusiasm for the director but a very clearly-articulated position vis-à-vis that director's legacy. One can see Chabrol's influence in a mystery film like Ozon's *Swimming Pool*, while Rohmer's mark is easily discernible in a verbose comedy of manners such as the late short *Un Lever de rideau* (which Ozon also compares to Godard's early comedy *Une Femme est une femme*), or in the final sequences of *5x2* and *Le Temps qui reste* (2005), both of which take place at seaside resorts. Ozon may draw, then, from rich and varied sources of inspiration both within France and internationally, but the end product is a distinctly singular one. In many ways, Ozon stands as a solitary figure among his own generation of French film directors, constantly changing hue, difficult to pin down. His films do not turn around the preoccupations of the bourgeois or bohemian intelligentsia in the manner of Arnaud Desplechin or Patrice Chéreau, but neither do they seek out working-class settings and issues in the manner of earthier filmmakers such as Robert Guédiguian or Bertrand Tavernier. Often avoiding realism altogether, Ozon's world is usually fantasy-fuelled; and yet his are fantasies many miles away from the beautifully dreamy, otherworldly landscapes of, say, Claire Denis. These fantasies instead inhabit a hybrid and sometimes unashamedly tacky space: real life soaked in a heady perfume of bad romantic fiction, musical melodrama and perhaps a little light pornography.

In the following three chapters I discuss Ozon's corpus in roughly chronological order, but I group the films according to the distinct ideological 'movements' I see occurring as his career progresses. Chapter 1 considers the majority of Ozon's short films together with his first feature *Sitcom* through the lens of desire, and demonstrates the extent to which Ozon's vision of human sexuality can be described as a fundamentally 'queer' and 'post-modern' one. The fluid and fluctuating character of the sexual identities these early films represent does not in itself promise to liberate their characters from their various comedic and dramatic shackles: the genuine subversions and transformations some of these films create must come from a place beyond sex. Chapter 2 considers four of Ozon's simultaneously most accomplished and misunderstood films – *Regarde la mer, Les Amants criminels, Gouttes d'eau sur pierres brûlantes* and *8 femmes* – and approaches them via the perspective of the power relations they depict. Suggesting that these films are again structured around an apparently flexible conception of dominance and submission, I again move on to argue that the superficial reversibility of sadomasochistic roles in which these films appear to revel in fact masks a far more intractable set of tensions and inequalities, impasses that can be exploded only by the films' indication of an (unthinkable) struggle outside the confines of master/servant terrain. Chapter 3 surveys a number of Ozon's films from the 2000s (*Sous le sable*, *Swimming Pool*, *5x2* and *Le Temps qui reste*), and claims that the earlier films' often (even if only ironically) 'progressive' transfigurations of subjectivity and relation beyond both sex and power are replaced in this later cycle by an essentially narcissistic vision of society and the self refracted through cinema. The final main chapter considers all of Ozon's output in the context of film genre. As well as simply pointing out the regularity with which his films utilise the rather unfashionable legacies of Hollywood horror, musical and melodrama in the forging of a peculiarly hybrid French cinema, I propose that Ozon's fondness for passage into these 'excessive' genres is often closely connected to an ongoing experimentation with the dynamics of over-stimulation and metamorphosis. To understand the significance of Ozon's cinema is to accept his early delight in the creation of worlds that veer suddenly and unexpectedly into the simply indigestible. This 'indigestibility' is experienced by character and spectator alike, and takes a variety of forms: leading ladies breaking into song-and-dance routines quite out of the blue in *8 femmes*; a sudden close-up of a toothbrush being dipped in human faeces in *Regarde la mer*; a mild-mannered father suddenly transforming into a giant rat in *Sitcom*. Ozon's experimentation with these 'jolts' within the cinematic experience are neither hollow nor merely provocative, but are instead inextricably linked to the potential transformation of the spectator. Drawn again and again to narrative situations wherein characters struggle to effect change or progress, trapped as they are within stiflingly circular psychic, social and familial dynamics, the younger Ozon employs alarming generic lurches within the gears of the films themselves in order to generate the electric shock necessary for both protagonist and viewer to snap out of their neurotic lethargy and simply take action.

As both Chapters 3 and 4 start to point out, then, while Ozon's brilliant series of shorts, as well as his first few feature films tend to hinge upon this exciting shift between addictive, anxiety-ridden, transgression-focused inertia and the passage into a truly unthinkable new state of active 'becoming', his films from *Sous le sable* onwards tend to keep characters and spectators alike trapped in an increasingly isolated and immobile dimension of fantasy. I do not propose an explicitly politicised reading of Ozon's filmic trajectory. I would nevertheless suggest that the reader may wish to consider Ozon's general turning away from the aesthetics of metamorphosis (metamorphosis that invariably involves the radical evacuation of spectrally paternal presences and culminates in the miraculous formation of new communities) and his gravitation towards ever more static explorations of the individual's paralysed desire within the historical context of chronic indifference at the heart of French society at the dawn of the twenty-first century. In 1995 Ozon made a sympathetic documentary (*Jospin s'éclaire*) about the French socialist presidential candidate Lionel Jospin. This was still a time when a belief in the possibility of a regenerated, radical left, uniting factions through the honest exorcism of colonial ghosts, remained a possibility in France, despite Jacques Chirac's ongoing presidency. Twelve years later, the right-wing former Minister of the Interior Nicolas Sarkozy was elected to the Elysée, a testament to the country's apparent acceptance of the triumph of a rampant individualistic neo-liberalism. Even if Ozon publicly spoke of the danger posed to the country by Sarkozy, over the period in which the climate for Sarkozy's presidential reception fully ripened, the gradual decline in the social possibilities opened up within the film-worlds he creates mirror, to an astonishing extent, France's increasing renunciation of the possibility of relation, revolution or community reborn.[2]

---

2 Ozon was one of a hundred stars of the arts and sciences who, in the run-up to the presidential elections of 2007, signed a petition supporting the candidacy of the socialist Ségolène Royal, a petition which claimed that 'to vote against Nicolas Sarkozy is to avoid the danger of a France at war with itself, in conflict and in crisis, divided and torn apart'. Other signatories included the writer Marie NDiaye, the actress Jeanne Moreau, the film director Constantin Costa-Gavras and the singer Georges Moustaki.

References

Hain, Mark (2007) 'Explicit Ambiguity: Sexual Identity, Hitchcockian Criticism, and the Films of François Ozon', *Quarterly Review of Film and Video*, 24: 277–88.

Internet sources

www.francois-ozon.com, accessed July 2007.

1

Desire unlimited: sexualities on the move?

Alongside filmmakers such as Catherine Breillat (*Romance*, 1999), Virginie Despentes (*Baise-moi*, 2000), Bruno Dumont (*Twentynine Palms*, 2003) Christophe Honoré (*Ma mère*, 2004) and Gaspar Noé (*Irréversible*, 2002), François Ozon has often been marketed and discussed – his surname serving the purpose particularly well – as one of a new breed of provocative French film directors emerging in the 1990s, all apparently preoccupied with pushing back the boundaries of sexual representation in mainstream cinema.[1] And indeed, from the early shorts of the mid-1990s to the ever-more polished features of the 2000s, Ozon's films often seem to delight in graphic images of unrestrained sexual activity. In *Victor* (1993) we see the eponymous hero masturbate himself to climax, his semen spurting all over his chest and chin. In *Action Vérité* (1994) Ozon shows us one teenage girl feel in jest between the legs of another, only to pull out a hand covered in menstrual blood. In *Les Amants criminels* (1999) the camera focuses on the face of the teenage hero as he is sodomised by a bearded 'ogre'. In 1998's *Sitcom* a candid medium-shot of the naked and erect penis of Stéphane Rideau being pushed between the breasts of Lucía Sánchez is served up unflinchingly for the spectator's delectation. It is small wonder that some critics have impatiently categorised Ozon as just one more director out to shock with trangressive sex.[2] Furthermore, Ozon's cinema is frequently discussed not as

1 The French verb 'oser' means 'to dare', leading to the first-person plural imperative 'Osons!' ('Let's dare!'), a homonym of 'Ozon'.
2 See, for example, Richard Falcon's article 'Reality is too shocking', in which the author dismissively states that Ozon's 1998 feature *Sitcom*, together with Lars von Trier's film *The Idiots*, 'hark back to the naïve belief held by audiences and

just sexual, but as specifically homosexual. Thus he has been categorised within a second, somewhat artificial set of directors – a putative
cinematic 'family' of French gay filmmakers that might include Jean
Cocteau (*Orphée*, 1950), Jean Genet, (*Un Chant d'amour*, 1950) André
Téchiné (*J'embrasse pas*, 1991) and the team of Olivier Ducastel and
Jacques Martineau (*Ma vraie vie à Rouen*, 2002), with the possible
inclusion of Cyril Collard (*Les Nuits fauves*, 1993) as a token bisexual.
Ozon's films, like those of the aforementioned, are shown as a matter
of course at international gay and lesbian film festivals, and it is to
such community-specific marketing that much of his success in the
English-speaking world can be attributed.[3] Again, such a 'ghettoisation' of Ozon might be said to be not wholly unreasonable. With some
notable exceptions, his films make visible images of homoeroticism,
trajectories of gay psychological development, and vagaries of gay
social experience with both an unabashed frankness and a refreshing
casualness. Whether via the shyly fellating male lovers of *Scènes de lit*
(1997), the enthusiastic sodomies of 1995's *La Petite Mort*, 1996's *Une
Robe d'été*, and 2005's *Le Temps qui reste*, or the unexpectedly numerous
all-star Sapphic couplings of 2002's *8 femmes*, Ozon conveys a world
in which same-sex desire is both irrepressible and seemingly ubiqui-
tous.[4]

---

filmmakers in the past that pushing the boundaries of notional good taste ...
could rock the status quo' (1999: 12).

3 Ozon's celebration as a specifically gay filmmaker has been particularly marked
in the United States: both *Une Robe d'été* and *Les Amants criminels* won prizes
at the Los Angeles Outfest Film Festivals of 1996 and 1999, while *Gouttes d'eau
sur pierres brûlantes* was named best feature at the 2000 New York Gay and
Lesbian Film Festival. According to Melvil Poupaud, the star of Ozon's 2005
film *Le Temps qui reste*, however, 'people in France don't think of Ozon as a gay
filmmaker. And they didn't think of this movie as a gay film ... Maybe we've
gotten over these things' (Duralde, 2006). As for Ozon himself, his position
vis-à-vis the question of ghettoisation is characteristically flippant but revealing:
'Je me fous de l'étiquette du cinéma pédé, même si ça me fatigue. Ce qui
m'énerve, c'est d'entendre des gens me dire: "Ras-le-bol de ces sujets-là!", alors
que bon, personne ne reproche à Claude Sautet de faire des films hétéros' ('I
don't give a shit about the queer cinema label, even if it tires me. What irritates
me is when I hear people tell me "We've had it up to here with those themes",
when, hey, nobody gives Claude Sautet a hard time for making straight films',
Doustaly, 1999).

4 An article such as 'Representations of homosexuality in 1990s mainstream
French cinema' (Johnston, 2002) makes clear, however, just how varied an
approach to gay matters has been adopted by various contemporary French film

While these attempts to approach Ozon's cinema through specifically sexual matrices are understandable starting points for analysis, they both demand a carefully nuanced application.[5] Sexual desire as represented by Ozon is almost always multidimensional and consistently astonishing (even to its own bearer) in its capacity for boundless reinvention. In 2005's *Le Temps qui reste*, the protagonist Romain speaks to his avuncular doctor of dreams that frame him as the lover of his own father, of the doctor himself, and, perhaps most intriguingly, of his own self in child form. Later in the film, he will impregnate a casually encountered waitress while her husband kisses and stimulates him.[6] Similarly, in 2004's *5x2*, in one of the film's many brutal expositions of the inscrutability of the central couple's 'true' desires, the clean-cut, apparently heterosexual husband and father Gilles publicly confesses (or invents?) his part in a sex party in the course of which he allegedly joined a married couple on the floor, penetrating the wife while being sodomised by the husband. Far from providing new sexual appellations or diagnoses with which to circumscribe their characters' behaviours, Ozon's films seem instead to revel in a more thoroughly generalised blurring of the very contours of desire, a blurring as pronounced in the construction of their female characters as in that of their male ones. In 1997's *Regarde la mer*, the first real sign that the rather repressed and exceedingly middle-class English housewife-and-mother protagonist Sasha has started to undergo characteristically Ozonian transformation is when she enters a forest of cruising gay men and proceeds to engage in cunnilingus with a random male figure. Charlotte Rampling's middle-aged English academic Marie in 2001's *Sous le sable* enjoys her one scene of orgasm as she masturbates to the fantasy (visually represented on-screen and thus shared by the spectator) of being caressed by

---

directors, some clearly more interested in practical/sociological issues such as gay parenting and civil partnerships than in theoretical questions of gender, desire and the construction of sexualities.

5 See Adam Bingham's (2003) article 'Identity and love: the not-so discreet charm of François Ozon', for a useful corrective to the often-made assumption that Ozon's films are 'about' homosexuality as such.

6 This image of the male protagonist unexpectedly enjoying sexual relations with both a man and a woman functions, it might be argued, as the quintessential leitmotif of Ozonian desire, the visitation in real terms of a 'primal scene' in which one's copulating parents are not only witnessed by the child, but are in fact joined by him.

several pairs of smooth male hands. Ozon's films and their numerous representations of sexual desire are best understood, then, neither as symptoms of specifically French *fin de millénaire* drives to shock audiences through explicitness, nor as ever-proliferating artefacts from a reassuringly established French gay male subculture. Instead, Ozon, like his American filmmaker contemporary Gregg Araki (born 1959), persistently disrupts his audience's expectations of what could possibly be meant by coherence of either sexuality or subjectivity. The two filmmakers (and they are clearly not the only ones) arguably belong less to nation-, gender- and sexuality-specific cinematic contexts than to a potentially international tendency, the legacy of intellectual and political struggles emerging from Europe and the Americas from the mid-1960s onwards, towards the constant affirmation of radically unmoored, provisional, and postmodern sexual behaviours, affiliations and identifications.[7] If Ozon's treatment of sex and sexualities *does* demand to be considered in the light of a specifically French history and culture of transgression, then it is perhaps more fruitful to compare him with a handful of French literary precursors than with his French cinematic contemporaries. Ozon's films explore ideas around radically 'unlawful' sexualities that are often reminiscent of writers like the Marquis de Sade (*La Philosophie dans le boudoir*, 1794), the Comte de Lautréamont (*Les Chants de Maldoror*, 1869), and Georges Bataille (*Histoire de l'œil*, 1928). Whether through the Sadeian trope of a secluded space within which a sexualised 'evil' may be enacted (rehearsed, for example, in a film like *Regarde la mer*), the Lautréamontian motif of a psychotic or fantastical dimension of sexualised being far beyond merely human transgression (as we see in *Sitcom*), or the Bataillean fascination with the existential implications of eroticised sacrifice (explored in *Les Amants criminels*), Ozon's analysis of mutating sexual desire is layered and nuanced in a manner that sharply interrogates the ethics of relation *tout court*, and certainly moves well beyond the superficiality of mere sexual spectacle.

7 The French student and worker uprisings of May–June 1968, the academic popularisation in the 1970s and 1980s of the philosophies of Gilles Deleuze and Michel Foucault and the increasing cultural currency from the 1990s onwards of the notion of 'queerness' – the refusal of all impositions of normative sexual labels – might all be cited as influences on the social and cinematic visions of Araki and Ozon. Kate Ince (2008) makes a case for considering Ozon as France's first mainstream queer director.

Sex and death *ad nauseam*: from *Victor* (1993) to *La Petite Mort* (1995)

Ozon's early films display a remarkable sophistication in their handling of the intersection of sexuality, transgression, death and their combined role in the shaping of the ever-metamorphosing human subject. He made the 13-minute film *Victor* in 1993, his graduating piece from the prestigious Paris film school FEMIS. Despite its brevity and the institutional context from which it emerged, it can be considered to be the first really polished prototype of Ozon's entire subsequent corpus of shorts and features, wrestling in witty and confident manner with social, ethical and psychoanalytic themes, character archetypes, and generic concerns that would dominate his films throughout the 1990s and 2000s. Ozon himself is rather dismissive about the piece, describing it as 'une étape utile mais aussi une sorte de carte de visite ... un exercice de style' ('a useful stage but in a business-card kind of way ... an exercise in style', Ozon official website, 'Interviews sur Les Courts- Métrages'). For all this, its plot details, narrative structure and *mise-en-scène* deserve detailed analysis: the very artificiality and brittleness by which Ozon seems embarrassed (and which would set some critics so strongly against *Sitcom*) may be precisely the source of its fable-like force. *Victor* shockingly and pithily asks a series of key, interlinked questions. How does one liberate oneself from one's parents and develop a truly adult subjectivity? How does one break out of a state of generalised stasis and begin to move forward? How does one discover and 'own' an autonomous sexual identity?

The film begins with a montage of black-and-white photographs of the eponymous hero, the baby-faced, post-adolescent Victor (François Genty), captured in stifling family shots, wedged tightly, infantilised in a grotesque manner, between austere-looking, middle-aged parents (Daniel Martinez and Martine Erhel). Elizabethan-style harpsichord music can be heard on the soundtrack. As the various photographs are displayed, we hear the voice of Victor reading out loud what sounds like the beginnings of a suicide note addressed to his 'chers parents' ('dear parents') and bemoaning his unworthiness as a son, whilst a succession of brief medium shots show him at his desk writing the letter in question. Victor then takes a revolver out of his desk drawer, and inserts it into his mouth. A woman in a maid's uniform (Isabelle Journeau) is busy in another room of the house, dusting one of the many household statues; outside in the garden an old man

(Jean-Jacques Forbin) toils, another white statue behind him. As the maid dusts, humming merrily while she works, a gunshot is heard. However, the subsequent shot, taking us to the source of the bang, via a leisurely pan down the Michelangelo-style fresco of the parents' bedroom, shows us not Victor's corpse but rather the cadavers of the parents, freshly killed by their son, who now sucks the long barrel of the gun in anticipation of his own imminent suicide. But before he has a chance to shoot himself in the mouth, he is interrupted by the cries outside the room of the maid, Julie. It is at this point that the film's title is shown, the word 'Victor' displayed in capital white letters in the middle of a gold photograph frame against a black background. The remaining eleven minutes of the film recount the next few days of Victor's life following the murder of his parents, as he embarks on a journey towards something like acceptance of both the parricide and of himself. It is to the aged gardener that he turns for guidance and reassurance, terrified by the situation he has brought about. Twice babbling a dementedly elliptical version of the horror that has occurred – 'J'ai un problème avec mes parents ... J'ai eu tellement peur de leur faire du mal que j'ai fait une autre chose ... mais tellement pire que ... !'('I have a problem with my parents...I was so afraid of hurting them that I did something else...but so much worse that ... !') – he receives from the old man only the same enigmatic and somewhat platitudinous speech about the necessity of waiting for things to work out for the best.[8] Victor is alone – albeit with two dead parents for constant company. He spends his days playing with the cadavers as though they were giant dolls: he combs his mother's hair as she sits slumped before her mirror; he sniffs his father's crotch in bed as he barks like a dog; he slurps soup (embarrassedly begging his parents' pardon) in the dining room with each corpse seated on either side of him.[9] A little later we see him lie masturbating to climax in the garden, while the dead parents sit slumped on the garden swings. Meanwhile, the maid Julie is beginning to exercise a new influence on the environment. Surreptitiously watching Victor's eccentric behaviour with his

8 The 'unspeakability' of Victor's original and subsequent sins, together with the empty indecipherability of the gardener's advice, function as empty spaces around which the absurd horrors of the narrative are framed.

9 Ozon frequently refers to his boyhood passion for dolls and doll's houses, and it is not difficult to see how his many of his films continue to enact that passion on a larger – and altogether more gruesome – scale.

parents, she is aware of everything that has happened. Having introduced her oafishly virile lover (Laurent La Basse) into the household,
she begins to steal, quite openly, the various clothes and valuables of the
deceased master and mistress. And when – in the film's most shockingly disturbing sequence – Victor is assaulted by the (psychotically
hallucinated?) reanimated 'zombie' figures of the parents, declaring
their fury at his continued transgressions and vowing punishment,
Julie and the lover take Victor into the bed in which he has already
witnessed them copulating *a tergo*, sandwiching him between their
naked bodies in a scene of overwhelmingly intimate, extreme close-ups
of flesh, hair, and unidentifiable body parts, out of the mass of which
Victor's large eyes poke.[10] The morning after Victor's sexual initiation,
Julie and the lover abruptly leave, driving away in Victor's parents' car,
adorned in the parents' expensive clothes, and waving cheerily up at
Victor who watches them from a grey, oval-shaped, upstairs window,
into which he then slips softly backwards.[11] Victor comes down to the
garden in his trousers and vest, and sets about burying his parents.
The gardener approaches, and Victor hands him the spade, declaring:
'Ils sont partis' ('they've gone away'). When the old man begins to
address Victor with his (by now) familiar speech of platitudes, Victor
silences him with a long, authoritative and intimate hug; the gardener
wordlessly reciprocates the gesture. The final frame is a long shot of
Victor: alone, still in white vest and black trousers, and smiling to
himself, he waits to board the Métro which is just arriving. The credits
play out over the barely discernible strains of 'Sometimes I Feel like
a Motherless Child'.[12]

10 The scene may allude to Freud's famous account of the 'Wolf Man', whose
   adult sexuality is traced to his childhood witnessing of his father's penetration
   of his mother from behind. In the same way, *Sitcom* could be viewed as a sort
   of cinematic adjunct to Freud's 'Rat Man' case study. Michelle Chilcoat (2007)
   analyses the parallels between the Freud case studies and Ozon's work at some
   length, and quotes Ozon's stated fondness for reading these texts.
11 Catherine and Suzon are framed within a very similar kind of window in a shot
   of *8 femmes*, shortly before the camera zooms inside to reveal the sisters in a
   regressed state of play, singing and clutching a teddy bear. The high oval window
   appears to function for Ozon as kind of symbolic interface between adulthood
   and babyhood.
12 It is difficult not to see this final detail as a musical nod to Pasolini's *The Gospel
   According to Saint Matthew* (1964). Ozon would later pay even more homage to
   the great Italian director via *Sitcom*'s liberal borrowings from Pasolini's *Theorem*
   (1968).

As a story about a naive young man's necessary departure from the desecrated family castle, his brutal entrance into the adult world, and the role played in his progress by a well-meaning old man philosopher, *Victor* in some ways plays like a 1990s cinematic version of Voltaire's eighteenth-century fairy tale *Candide* and Flaubert's nineteenth-century saint's life *La Légende de Saint Julien L'Hospitalier* combined. It sets the stage for our understanding of Ozon as an *auteur* who is clearly fascinated by the ethics, the violence, the mysticism of coming of age, an *auteur* utterly willing to appropriate the aesthetics of the modern *conte*, or tale (at the expense of any kind of realism) in order to conduct his ahistorical investigations. *Victor* may be Ozon's 'student film', then, but it offers us a bold and unambiguous insight into the themes that structure the Ozonian universe. At one level, the film and its fable of parricide can be read as a gruesome joke about the potential horrors of 'coming out' as gay. We can infer that Victor wants, in the first instance, to kill himself because he cannot face what his parents would think, say, or do if he told them about his homosexuality. Ozon offers us various, not particularly subtle, clues that this may be the case. François Genty's performance as Victor is delivered throughout in a high-pitched, effeminate whine, characteristic of stereotypical representations of the male 'invert'. The unworthiness for which Victor upbraids himself in the putative suicide note is never specified, of course, but it is hardly an excessive move or over-interpretation on the part of the viewer to understand it as a reference to that much-discussed desire that 'dare not speak its name'. The entire film is suffused in an atmosphere of barely suppressed homoeroticism. The gazes of both Victor and the spectator are, for example, directed to alight on Julie's male lover rather than on Julie herself. When the lover is first introduced he is shown in medium shot, from behind, urinating against a tree. Victor watches from a lowered position in rapt fascination (he has been crawling through the grass, gathering dead leaves). The following low-angle, point-of-view shot of the lover's gruff, stupidly confident stare, his mane of dark hair framed by trees and blossom, his white vest stretched tightly over a huge chest, and large bicep and tufts of underarm hair occupying about one-fifth of the frame, conspires to make this entire spectacle of manhood stare down at both Victor and the spectator, cementing the latter into the former's worshipful subjectivity and desire. A broadly homoerotic aesthetic sets in from this point onwards, with the lover frequently captured from behind, the spectator forced to drink him in as the object of Victor's desiring gaze. In the scene where Victor catches him ransacking his parents' bedroom for jewels, the lover partially – and quite gratuitously – strips in order to put on a coat, allowing both Victor and the spectator to gaze at Laurent La Basse's chest, torso and comically wiggling behind as he tortuously takes off the white vest (which Victor will then sniff longingly). And when, in another scene, Victor spies on the couple having sex, it is (by virtue of the nature of the kind of sex taking place) the male posterior that we are shown in full view, not that of Isabelle Journeau, whose body remains totally obscured from the camera's view by that of the naked La Basse.

It would, however, be highly simplistic to wrap up *Victor*'s analysis of sexuality as that of a homoerotic short about the putative difficulties of 'coming out of the closet'. The very premise upon which the film is based – that Victor should: (a) shoot both his parents rather than confess his sexual identity to them; (b) live and play with their cadavers; and (c) eventually leave the family home in a kind of triumph – is symptomatic of Ozon's ability to lift his narrative out of the banal circumscriptions of everyday discourses around sexuality, and onto a more radical plane of ethical inquiry. The violent murder with which the film begins can, provided we read it not so much as a literal exhortation to parricide as Ozon's first exercise in providing representational frameworks within which to inscribe radical processes of auto-therapy, be read as an extremely positive first step for our hero. In killing his parents, the obscenely infantilised Victor attempts to annihilate his parents' judging consciousnesses rather than his own. Victor's decision to turn the gun on the potentially judging parent, rather than become complicit in his own dissolution, represents something of an advance in terms of filial agency.[13] Read in this way, the closing bars of 'Sometimes I Feel like a Motherless Child' (a tune Victor also whistles halfway through the film as he swings next to his dead parents) take on the air less of a tragically lonely lament than of a radically post-familial victory song. Still, even this reading of *Victor*'s

13 The unworthy-offspring protagonist of the literature which Ozon's 'accursed family' cinema so often oddly calls to mind usually gets stuck in purely self-destructive mode: consider Gregor Samsa, Kafka's disintegrating beetle hero of *The Metamorphosis* (1915), or the unforgettable literary creation of Ozon's French contemporary Marie NDiaye, whose spurned heroine Fanny in the novel *En famille* (1990) ends up, through her own complicity with her family's various fascistic edicts, a dematerialising mess in the garden shed.

narrative trajectory fails to do justice to the complexity of Ozon's vision of the challenge of attaining an autonomous sexual subjectivity. For what the film really seems to take as its central subject matter is the manner in which the initial act of potentially 'positive' transgression – Victor shooting his parents instead of himself – utterly fails to inject into his life anything like progress or empowerment. For Victor – and here he is the template for nearly all Ozon's future protagonists – is neurotically bound by a desire to perform before parental bodies of authority, even when those bodies are silent, indifferent or even dead. Victor's various 'games' with his parents' corpses – slurping and belching in front of them at the dinner table, barking and snarling at them like a dog, sniffing his dead father's crotch – are presented as so many absurd attempts to provoke those corpses into some kind of impossible reaction. The film operates as an obscene comedy, then, spinning around this series of 'shocking' sketches, but beneath the laugher quietly swells the film's insistent repetition of a key and non-negotiable idea: Victor can do absolutely nothing to provoke parental acknowledgement of his subjective presence: his actions, no matter how transgressive, count for nothing. Symptomatic of all this is the old gardener's absolute refusal to recognise that Victor has done anything wrong, even though Victor implores him to listen to a confession. In the same way, the maid Julie and her lover are obviously, farcically aware of the double murder, but display an utterly amused indifference to it. Instead of movement, response or reaction, the film, its situations and its characters are immersed in images of silence, stagnation and stasis. From the film's very outset Ozon shows us family photographs intercut with shots of garden statues. The dead parents' rigor mortis is set up as a great comic tool, but functions also as an index of their maddeningly simultaneous rigidity and impassiveness. The repetition of identical dialogues between Victor and the gardener is both the stuff of absurd vaudeville and the nightmarish material of a relation that refuses to move forward.

If the film *does* beat out some kind of path out of this impasse, this emerges neither from its apparent revelry in homoerotic aesthetics nor from its seemingly ghoulish celebration of Victor's parricide, but rather from its gradual revelation and development of the new on-screen relations that develop from both. The sequence of events that propels Victor out of the 'haunted house' and into the outside world begins when Victor is confronted by the suddenly reanimated corpses of the parents who rise up in bed, zombie-like, and angrily castigate him for his outrageous behaviour. The 'horror film' dimensions and aesthetics of this sequence will be analysed at greater length in Chapter 4. What is important to note here is simply that this terrifying, fantastical, ultimately unreadable moment of the film acts as a far more effective shock to Victor's stultified psyche than did the initial, now utterly banal parricide. By the same token, the subsequent sexual encounter Victor enjoys with Julie and the lover – impossible to qualify in conventional terms of sexual preference – can be said to kick-start his adult subjectivity and agency in ways both masturbation and openly homosexual desire have thus far failed to do. Trapped between the lover and Julie – the lover kissing his neck while Victor plays with Julie's breasts – Victor finds himself in the act of actualising, in hitherto unthinkable form, the father–mother–Victor scenario around which he has structured his life thus far, but has never had the opportunity to make concretely sexual. The three-way scene's development into a situation of visual incomprehensibility, with only Victor's eyes visible amid a tangle of de-subjectified hair and limbs represents, like the parent-zombie scene, an essentially illegible expression of (sexual) experience, whose very visual lack of coherence appears to facilitate Victor's passage towards a truly new stage of desire and existence. *Victor* is important in the understanding of Ozon's early work, then, in its unashamed exposure of the way in which the young *auteur* turns to outlandish images that border on ridiculousness – dead parents coming back to life, a boy-child smothered and 'in pieces' between the naked bodies of his servants – in order to generate the electric shocks needed to push his film into new aesthetic and philosophical territory. The film's two shock images, its quasi-horrific, quasi-pornographic 'money shots' are what actualise the character Victor's repressed and impossible desires – to be scolded by parents in the form of monsters; to be present at the scene of 'parents' as they copulate – and are what enable him in narrative terms to pick up his spade the next morning, and start digging his parents' grave. *Victor* reveals Ozon, then, as a director unafraid to create flagrantly indigestible images on film in order to 'unblock' the stasis of both his characters and his spectators and put them in charge of their own post-parental destiny.

Ozon made the 26-minute film *La Petite Mort* in 1995, and it can, in many ways, be read as a longer and less grotesque exploration of the themes already raised by *Victor*. Ozon himself is even more dismissive of the work than he is of *Victor*, criticising it for its apparently 'obscene' sincerity.[14] An alternative view might suggest that the short film manages to convey a remarkable candour regarding the pain felt by the adult child in the face of the father's perceived indifference, via an overwrought emotional sensibility that runs throughout, and functions as the film's aesthetic 'intensifier' in the same way as horror does in *Victor*. The plot is as follows: Paul (played with a wonderfully petulant, bug-eyed, tearful directness by François Delaive), a nervy, twenty-something photographer, lives with his calm, kindly, muscle-bound boyfriend Martial (Martial Jacques). Paul is obsessed with his latest artistic project, which consists of photographing men in the throes of masturbatory orgasm. His and Martial's apartment is adorned with the black-and-white faces of these men, in whose beatific expression of climax Paul hopes to capture something like an image of the sublime.[15] Paul's already anxious temperament and ill humour towards Martial is aggravated by the fact that his father (Michel Beaujard), from whom he has been estranged for years, is dying, while his equally uptight sister Camille (Camille Japy) constantly berates him for a perceived lack of filial responsibility. Finally agreeing to visit the dying father, Paul is disappointed beyond words when the latter fails to recognise him. Plunging back into his photography project, he decides to combine the two major preoccupations of his life by returning surreptitiously to the hospital where the father lies dying, stripping the father naked while he sleeps, and taking a handful of photographs of the corpse-like body before being discovered by a horrified Camille, who ejects him in disgust. Back at home, Paul develops the photographs of his father in his darkroom, discovering in the process that the father's wide open and staring eyes have been captured on film, despite the old man's sleeping

14 'Je n'aime pas beaucoup ce film parce qu'il me semble trop scénarisé et trop bouclé ... Avec le temps, la volonté de sincérité et de mise à nu du film me paraît un peu obscène. Il y a certainement des choses de moi que je n'ai pas forcément envie de voir' ('I don't much care for this film, finding it excessively script-led and shut-down ... With the passage of time, the film's drive for sincerity and laying things bare starts to strike me as somewhat obscene. There are definitely things about me in it that I don't necessarily want to see', Ozon official website, 'Interviews sur Les Courts-Métrages').

15 The 'little death' of the title is an expression which in French refers to sexual climax, stemming from the idea that in orgasm human consciousness is obliterated in an ecstatic state not unlike a death from which one returns.

appearance. Paul cuts out the eyes, and puts on his father's uncanny death mask, moving his own eyes around within it in a kind of astonished triumph. Receiving news of his father's death some time later, Paul is able to make tearful love to Martial for the first time since the film's start. A montage of black-and-white images of photographed male bodies is shown rather than Paul and Martial themselves. Paul meets Camille in a café, where she berates him for not attending his father's funeral, but also tells him that their father had been happy to be photographed by his son in his last days. The two siblings, in a moment of tearful honesty, reconcile their differences, and Camille gives Paul some photographs that their father had wanted him to have. Alone at the Métro station, Paul looks at a photograph of himself as a baby, cradled in his father's arms. Light blue fills the screen.

As is the case with *Victor*, or a film like the much later *Le Temps qui reste* (2005), *La Petite Mort* runs the risk of being read in a superficial manner as a 'gay' film. Featuring an overtly homosexual male protagonist, explicit sequences of gay sex and numerous shots of the muscular Martial Jacques lounging around in nothing but a towel, the film seems to dare the spectator to limit and categorise it as such, before it joyfully leaps to confound such an attempt. Like *Victor*, *La Petite Mort* revolves instead around the idea that adult sexuality is anything but resolved just because the adult in question has chosen a partner. And this lack of resolution does not derive from a conventionally understandable hesitation – the bisexual wavering, say, between a male or female lover – but rather from the maddening sensation within the perturbed subject that neither sexual identity nor subjective cohesion *tout court* are attainable goals. Paul's relation with Martial is, for the most part, one characterised by an absence of rapport, rather than an easy and comprehensible sexual fusion.[16] From the film's outset, masturbation rather than intercourse is posited as the sexual act par excellence, as Paul instructs Martial to photograph him in the

16 The psychoanalyst Jacques Lacan encapsulates the futility of a romantic belief in a direct connection or interplay, unmediated by fantasy, between the desires of two heterosexual lovers with his much-quoted phrase 'il n'y a pas de rapport sexuel' – 'there is no sexual relationship' (1975: 17). In a situation like the one evoked by Paul and Martial, Ozon extends the observation into homosexual territory, making clear that it is sexual difference *tout court*, sexual difference between all subjects and within all subjects, not merely the sexual differences between those categorised as 'men' and 'women', that renders impossible a satisfied two-way sexual relation, inscribed in a naturally occurring plenitude.

throes of orgasm. He will later pin the resulting photograph over an old photograph of himself as a baby. An uneasy narcissism and the desire to desire himself are the activities that consume Paul's drives in this film, both preoccupations bypassing everyday categorisations of sexual preference. It soon becomes apparent that Paul's overriding problem is the deeply rooted feeling that he does not deserve to exist as such. Like the pathetic little Victor, who, just before that film's closing scenes shouts 'Je suis là!' ('I'm here!') from the turret of his grey oval window frame at the fast disappearing Julie and the lover, Paul is condemned to an irrational conviction that he is illegitimate to the point of radical alienation. His voiceover, as the film begins, over a still black-and-white image of a photograph of a newborn baby, tells us that when his father, away on business, was sent a picture of his new son, he replied that this 'monstre' could not be his son: it was too ugly. Later, at the hospital, the father will once again find it beyond his capabilities to recognise his son. As if to hammer the point home, on the train on the way home from that visit Paul will be unable to produce his identity card when asked to, having mistakenly put on the jeans of his boyfriend.

The photographs of orgasm – both his own and that of innumerable other men – that Paul strives so hard to produce would seem to derive, then, from a need to give solid form to a fleeting, evanescent sensation of existence, to capture on film, in 'over-present', pornographic form, the proof that he and others do in fact live and feel. When Martial, with a mocking lasciviousness, points out to a disgusted Camille the drops of semen that can be glimpsed on his cheek in his own wall portrait, he sums up much of Ozon's own apparent preoccupation with embodiment and incarnation: like Paul (via Martial's semen), Ozon (via instances of fantastical monstrosity, excessive emotionalism, illegible obscenity and improbable musicality) is fascinated with film's unreal capacity for capturing (or feigning) the concrete, material traces (or externalisations) of ecstatic (or traumatic) experience. And yet, for all Paul's photographic attempts to 'move on', the film, like *Victor*, is mired in *topoi* of stillness and stagnation. This film too begins with the image of a still photograph, and that initial stillness contaminates the atmosphere of the characterisations, narrative and *mise-en-scène* that follows. Paul is caught in a static, uncommunicative, and lonely relationship not only with the well-meaning Martial, but also with his frustrated sister Camille. The film's structure lends support to the view – quite contrary to conventional narratives of sexual 'maturation', dependent as these usually are on a character's resolution with either the parent or the lover or both – that Paul's impasse with Camille is at least as pertinent to his existential morass as are his (non-) relations with Martial and the father. Camille Japy's performance oozes a statue-like paralysis, the scene where a dripping wet Martial attempts to kiss her cheeks and she freezes, arms folded, grimace immobile, serving as a perfect emblem of her static state of being. As for François Delaive as Paul, his gestures are consistently jerky, strained, anything but fluid. Paul, like Victor, is caught, for the first half of the film, in a process of endless repetition. The numerous photographs of different men performing the same masturbatory performance for his character exemplify the character's doomed quest for the 'truth' of his sexuality and subjectivity, which finds any prospect of progress diverted towards motion in a neurotically circular movement.

If Victor first shoots his parents in a misguided attempt to move forward, then sniffs his dead father's crotch while barking like a dog, in this more realistic world of *La Petite Mort* Paul translates his attempted transgressions first into a self-conscious renunciation of his father, then a quasi-rape by camera of the old man as he lies naked and dying on a hospital bed. As both Ozon's and Paul's cameras linger in shocking close-up on the father's drip-filled arms, his white chest hair, and his wrinkled genitalia, the viewer is overwhelmed by the excessive violence of the scene and of Paul himself. Yet for all that violence the stasis of the situation remains intact: Paul stares wide-eyed and puppet-like at a hysterically furious Camille, repeating childish taunts, and, later, lies corpse-like and unresponsive in bed with Martial, refusing the latter's overtures of tenderness. Violence of this kind is not enough to push things forward. The film only tenta-tively sketches out an indication of potential motion for its protago-nist. Early in the film, as Martial explains to Camille the context of the men's expressions on the photographs on the wall, Ozon shows us several stills of the same man in rapid succession, creating an effect of almost 'live' motion as we watch the man's features change expres-sion and his eyes open wide. This moment in the film operates as a tiny spark of potential reanimation of dead matter.[17] Like the sudden

17 There exist a number of recent English-language inquiries into the ethical and aesthetic significance of the still versus the moving image within the context of cinema, all of which could be fruitfully placed in conjunction with an analysis

motion of the improbably prone zombie parents of *Victor*, the oddly moving unknown masturbator takes on an unforeseen form of life through an unexpected cessation of stillness. In the same way, when Paul later puts on his father's death mask and stares out of this new skin, wide-eyed and uncannily transformed, what we witness is essentially the quasi-magical metamorphosis of the 'dead' photograph of the father into a new hybrid Paul–father creature. In terms of the film's narrative structure, it seems important that it is only after this strange scene of reanimation that reconciliations of a kind will occur for Paul with Martial, then Camille, and finally the memory of his now truly dead father. While, as with *Victor*, the film's final scene of the young man alone at the Métro station is permeated by a certain wistful ambivalence, it might be argued that the logic of *La Petite Mort* is nevertheless guardedly optimistic, positing a potential transformation of neurotic subjectivity and a maturation of paralysed sexuality through neither the embracing of a new identity, however oppositional, nor through the performance of acts of transgression, but rather through the apparently 'unthinkable' donning of new skins and the willing entrance into truly new configurations of the self.

Adventures with a *femme fatale*: from *Une Rose entre nous* (1994) to *Une Robe d'été* (1996)

The two shorts *Une Rose entre nous* (27 minutes, 1994) and *Une Robe d'été* (15 minutes, 1996) explore the challenge to grow via the unforeseen exposure to radically new experiences of one's own desire and subjectivity in a far lighter manner than either *Victor* or *La Petite Mort*. Avoiding issues of death and violence altogether, these playful films instead focus on their (again, male) protagonists' progression within an exclusively – and thus potentially less strikingly – sexual framework, constructed in each case around an unexpected encounter with a kind of ironic *femme fatale*. And yet, again, a close examination of both films reveals that despite appearing merely to embody a kind of fashionably postmodern, bisexual mobility, the heroes of these narratives in fact undergo far more profound oscillations of social

---

of this particularly arresting sequence of *La Petite Mort*. See, for example, the article on Chris Marker's 1962 film *La Jetée* (ffrench, 2005), or *Death 24x a Second: Stillness and the Moving Image* (Mulvey, 2006).

positioning in the course of their transformational adventures. They illustrate, once again, that, in Ozon's world, not only is sexual identity not fixed, but that the social context, implications and repercussions of its unmooring are the points of interest, not just the unmooring itself. Ozon himself seems to prefer the apparent lightness of touch these films exude as compared with *Victor* and *La Petite Mort*, reporting particularly favourably on his lack of disappointment with *Une Robe d'été*: 'C'est la première fois que le résultat est aussi proche de mes intentions de narration et de sensations. C'est un film, comme je le souhaitais, joyeux et coloré sur la période de l'été, qui met en scène l'ambivalence sexuelle de l'adolescence, sans culpabilité' ('It's the first time the result comes so close to how I'd intended the narration and sensations to be. It's a happy, colourful, summery film, just as I'd wanted, framing the sexual ambivalence of teenage years in a guilt-less way', Ozon official website: Interviews sur les Courts-Métrages). Clearly Ozon was not the only one to feel this way, since *Une Robe d'été* proved a huge hit at the year's international film festivals, carrying home a clutch of prizes and propelling Ozon towards the important next phase of his career.

In *Une Rose entre nous*, the young hairdresser Paul (Rodolphe Lesage), visibly irritable around his overtly gay colleague Rémy (Christophe Hémon), is asked one morning by a mysterious young English-woman, Rose (Sasha Hails), if he can dye her hair 'roux comme un écureuil' ('red like a squirrel'). Upon his completion of the command Rose screams in fury, pretending never to have asked for such a thing, and storms out of the salon. Chasing after the beguiling woman, Paul is soon seduced by her charm. Agreeing to meet her that night outside what turns out to be a gay nightclub, Paul finds himself reluctantly drawn into Rose's plan for each of them to prostitute themselves separately to two rather unattractive older men, Robert (Jacques Disses) and Yves (Francis Arnaud). Back at Robert's house, Rose ecstatically performs cabaret songs for the three men, in stockings and suspenders, before going to bed with Robert and pushing Paul off with Yves. But while in the subsequent sequence we see Rose firmly refuse to have sex with Robert, and turn over to go to sleep, Paul keeps his part of the deal and has sex – his first time with a man, possibly with anyone – with Yves. Learning inadvertently from Yves that Rose has lied to him about the amount of money that has actually been paid for his favours, Paul confronts Rose in violent fury, but eventually agrees to go back with her to her apartment, where the two – Rose now softer and more giving – have reconciliatory sex. Paul tells Rose he is just going down to the street momentarily for croissants but, having bought the croissants, never returns, instead going straight to the salon, where he clowns with his colleague Rémy in a delighted spirit of happiness.

In *Une Robe d'été* glum teenager Luc (Frédéric Mangenot) is becoming increasingly exasperated with the hilariously overstated camp manner of his boyfriend Sébastien (Sébastien Charles, Ozon's regular choreographer), with whom he is on a seaside holiday. Leaving their rented apartment in irritation, he goes alone to swim naked in the sea. Waking up on the beach he meets a mysterious Spanish girl (Lucía Sánchez), who asks him for a light, then suggests they go to the woods to have sex. Agreeing in somewhat astonished amusement, Luc has apparently enjoyable sex with the girl, despite the fact that it is his first heterosexual experience, and that he has the perturbing sense that a strange man is watching them. Returning to the beach where they have left their things, Luc finds to his outrage that all his clothes have been stolen, while the girl's possessions remain untouched. She offers to lend him her colourful summer dress while she goes home in her bathing costume, a proposition he accepts with severe reluctance, agreeing that it is the only alternative to returning home naked. Once back at the holiday flat, Luc seems capable of flirting with a new-found ease with Sébastien, who immediately has sex with him, penetrating him on the kitchen table, and ripping the summer dress in the frenzied process. The next morning, in calm and tender repose with Sébastien, Luc mends the ripped dress with a needle and thread, and goes to the harbour to return it to the Spanish girl, who is about to leave on a boat with her parents. She tells him she is giving him the dress as a present, since it might come in handy in the future. They embrace tenderly, to the (extra-diegetic) tune of Sheila's song 'Bang Bang', the endless (intra-diegetic) performance of which by Sébastien had driven Luc out of the holiday home in the first place.

The two films have remarkably similar narrative structures, even if they differ substantially in tone and finesse, *Rose* being markedly more ragged and uneven than the shorter, slicker, pithier *Robe*.[18] The

18 Ozon himself, when comparing the films, seems to locate the fault of *Rose* in the performance of the leads, going so far as to say that Hails's acting here (as opposed to her later performance in *Regarde la mer*) 'part un peu dans tous

titles even echo one another, placing a similar sounding indefinite feminine object at the centre of affairs, the catalyst for the transformation of the male protagonist. In each film we find a sexually ambivalent boy, putatively heterosexual in the case of Paul, putatively homosexual in the case of Luc, who undergoes experiences in the course of events that will push him towards sexual activity he had hitherto considered unthinkable. In each case the boy hero moves from a jumpy, insecure, defensive stance vis-à-vis overt displays of 'gayness' in the opening frames to a relaxed, smiling, accepting posture of openness in the final shot. True to Ozonian form, though, this journey is not some tidily reversed version of the traditional passage from 'infantile' to 'mature' sexuality, presenting a happy homosexuality as the goal that is attained after a period of fluctuation. Instead, the stance of calm acceptance that characterises both Paul and Luc at the end of each film is difficult to ascribe to a resolved or clear-cut alignment with any particular sexual identity, merely to a renunciation of the fear and hostility they had previously shown towards overtly marginal forms of sexuality, here characterised by 'camp'. In both films the process of the hero's development is shown rather to be dependent upon sex both with a woman (foreign, mysterious, powerful, manipulative and knowing) capable of somehow 'feminising' him, *and* with another man who will literally penetrate him.

It is Paul's and Luc's loss of the vestiges of conventionally active masculinity that is at stake in these films, then, a loss that is brought about by a combination of both homosexual and heterosexual activity. The enforced and increasing passivity of both young men is insisted upon in all manner of ways. From the outset, the mysterious women they meet manipulate and control them in truly classic *femme fatale* style. The way in which these women address them is infantilising and desexualising: Rose constantly calls Paul 'mon petit frère' ('my little brother') and 'mon petit lapin' ('my little rabbit'), while the Spanish girl addresses Luc as 'mon enfant' ('my child'). But whereas in conventional Hollywood film noir the hero's emasculation by the *femme fatale* is met with increasing rage and debilitation, in these films the hero positively blooms under such de-virilising influence. And whereas in conventional film noir the hero's 'penetration' by

---

les sens' ('goes all over the place'), and strongly criticising (again, somewhat unfairly), the male lead in particular (Ozon official website: 'Interviews sur les Courts-Métrages').

the second (usually older) male character is alarming even though purely metaphorical, in these films both Paul and Luc will not only be literally sodomised by other men shortly after their meeting of the *femme*, but will both be more than capable of a smile after the event.[19] Luc's passive encounter, in particular, is conveyed as a liberated and ecstatic experience. Both boys are persuaded by the *femme fatale* to take on conventionally feminine roles and attributes. Paul becomes a whore for a night (in contrast to Rose herself, who remains tightly in control of her body), while the dress foisted upon Luc by the Spanish girl forces him into a comically striking transvestism. What is crucial about both these enforced feminisations, though, is their ephemeral nature. The summer dress, in particular, works in the film as a strikingly visual symbol of provisional identity, an item of clothing that drastically alters Luc's social positioning (cars beep at him as he cycles home) and sexual relations with Sébastien, able to be put on, ripped, taken off, mended and put on again, but altering the wearer's subjectivity in a lasting manner each time he engages with it.[20] The Spanish girl's giggles of knowing amusement as she hands him the dress, together with her smile of wise generosity when she gives it to him for keeps, make of her almost a divine agent of Luc's transformation.[21]

Both films are, then, shot through with an exuberant sense of flexibility and endless possibility for adaptation, change and reinvention. As Ozon himself has suggested, *Une Robe d'été* in particular is so pleasing because of its joyous reflection of a state of being no longer tormented by guilt and interdictions, but instead open to a limitless potentiality. Both films use a 'camp' sensibility not to insist upon the fixed nature of gay modes of being, but as the vehicle of a contagious type of behaviour that can 'infect' anyone, pushing him or her towards

19 Examples of classic Hollywood film noir 'triangles' include Billy Wilder's *Double Indemnity* (1944), with Fred MacMurray (as the 'boy') Barbara Stanwyck (as the *femme*) and Edward G. Robinson (as the older man), or Jacques Tourneur's *Out of the Past* (1947), with Robert Mitchum, Jane Greer and Kirk Douglas in that configuration.

20 Britt-Marie Schiller (2005) discusses the transformation-by-dress of the much later 'masculine' (though, in fact, female) Ozon character, Sarah Morton (Charlotte Rampling) in comparable terms in her psychoanalysis of Ozon's film *Swimming Pool* (2003).

21 The heavily accented Lucía Sánchez is rather reminiscent of the supernatural Princess/Death as played by Maria Casarès in Cocteau's 1950 film of *Orphée*: both are raven-haired and commanding southern seductresses who effortlessly will a sexually ambivalent 'hero' to follow them faithfully over to 'the other side'.

exuberantly performative acts and relations that split and multiply the self into myriad fragments of ironic, self-referential cultural material. Thus the song 'Bang Bang' by the 1960s French so-called gay icon Sheila operates in *Une Robe d'été* as a gleefully insidious germ, merrily spread by the dancing Sébastien until it is implanted not only in Luc's desire (he sings it as he is being sodomised) but also in the film's extra-diegetic soundtrack. In *Rose*, Paul's gay hairdresser colleague Rémy flits through the film as a quasi-spectral force, popping up briefly at the club where Paul and Rose dance, and, in the film's final frames, melting, mobilising, dynamising Paul's initial immobile rigidity and stiffness at least as much as Rose and Yves put together. As for femininity itself, both the films seem determined to present it as a floating signifier of pure artifice, even (or perhaps especially) when displayed by a biological female. The English Rose and the Spanish temptress perform their identities from start to finish: it is impossible to tell where their tricks and ruses stop and where 'they' begin. Both seem addicted to lying: Rose's untruths are legion, while the Spanish girl's initial request for a light is later revealed as pure pretext. Rose's name screams out to be read as a tongue-in-cheek falsehood, a clichéd appeal to the fantasies of Englishness to which the men she encounters may be susceptible. Her changing hair colour seems (like that of 'Tippi' Hedren in Hitchcock's *Marnie*) to function as an index of her changing temperament and agenda; the opening shot of the rose tattoo on her back hammers home her commitment to making her body into a mere bearer of signs. Both women are strange combinations of *femme fatale* and fairy-tale enchantress, leading the hero into the woods (literally, in the case of Luc) to have his identity shredded.[22] These anti-heroines, as played by the Englishwoman Sasha Hails and the Spanish actress Lucía Sánchez respectively, are the first examples

22 That these 'postmodern' female spiders, these 'parodic' phallic women, lead their boys into a kind of chaos that, within the ethics of the films themselves, is ultimately somehow redemptive, is interestingly inventive, but remains problematic, I would suggest, for truly feminist representation. For these women figures are still, in the final analysis, utterly dispensable, ladders to be kicked away once the hero has learned from the transgressions she offers. Ozon's representation of women seems stuck in these early films at a certain level of simplicity. We will need to ask ourselves the question of whether later, more 'female-oriented' narratives such as *8 femmes* or *Swimming Pool* manage to bestow autonomy and humanity upon their women characters with any greater degree of success.

of Ozon's ongoing fascination (rather in the manner of Jean-Luc Godard) with foreign actresses playing in French.[23] Putting on and taking off the French language as a kind of linguistic drag, slipping into their mother tongues at moments when they feel the greatest need to charm and confuse, they reveal that language, like sex, is just one more category of being that it is easy to slip between – and with constantly surprising results – once you know how.

Sex, laughs and a rat on a platter: *Sitcom* (1998)

Ozon's most explicitly sex-centred film of this, or indeed any, period, is the seven-sketch short *Scènes de lit* (1997). Despite an impressive range of situations, it is all too apparent that it is a film made because, as Ozon himself puts it, 'je m'ennuyais et [que] j'avais envie de tourner' ('I was bored and I wanted to shoot something', Ozon official website: Interviews sur les Courts-Métrages). Slickly amusing the sketches may be, but the 26-minute film as a whole carries an aesthetic superficiality and intellectual vacuity that is disagreeably surprising in the context of a period in which the twenty-something Ozon was churning out shorts that – despite the appearance of superficiality and vacuity – were, in fact, consistently groundbreaking in their depth and sophistication.[24] Ozon's first feature, on the other hand, the 1998 film *Sitcom*, will stand – despite, or perhaps because of, some of the scathing and incensed reviews it provoked upon its release – as one

---

23 Hails reappears in *Regarde la mer* and Sánchez in *Sitcom*. Other examples of foreign female protagonists in Ozon's French-language films include Anna Thomson in *Gouttes d'eau sur pierres brûlantes* and Charlotte Rampling in *Sous le sable* and *Swimming Pool*.

24 The seven *Scènes de lit* are as follows: (a) 'Le Trou noir' – a soldier (François Delaive) visits a prostitute (Valérie Druguet) to sample her speciality: fellatio while singing 'La Marseillaise'; (b) 'Monsieur Propre' – a couple's first night of passion is spoiled by the man's boasting of his own lack of hygiene; (c) 'Madame' – an older woman picks up a younger man and they wonder how to proceed; (d) 'Tête bêche' – a couple lies top-to-tail in bed, counting backwards (she in Spanish, he in French) from 100 to 69; (e) 'L'Homme idéal' – a woman counsels her younger friend after romantic disappointment, before seducing her herself; (f) 'L'Amour dans le noir' – a couple quarrel over whether or not to have the lights out during sex; (g) 'Les Puceaux' – two young men lie in bed and discuss their opposing virginities, the one a stranger to homosexuality, the other to heterosexuality.

of the most shockingly inventive feature debuts of twentieth-century French cinema. The Ozonian filmic essay par excellence on the possibilities and impossibilities of non-normative desire, *Sitcom* burst onto French cinema screens like a weird cocktail of Buñuel's *Journal d'une femme de chambre* (1964), Pasolini's *Theorem* (1968), John Waters's *Pink Flamingos* (1972) and most of Pedro Almodóvar's output of the 1980s. An outrageous tendency towards a schlock-horror aesthetic adds an oddly David Cronenberg-like dimension into the mixture. Reviews of the film were extremely mixed, though, many critics feeling that Ozon's passage to feature-length had revealed a glaring lack of maturity together with a pitiful absence of originality.[25] What elevates *Sitcom* far above the status of merely clever pastiche, though, is the fact that Ozon carefully constructs all this homage around the utterly lucid, singular and thoroughgoing analysis – becoming increasingly clear as specifically Lacanian in bent – of desire, drive and identity that his early shorts had merely pointed towards.[26]

Sitcom tells the story of a middle-class suburban French family – housewife-mother Hélène (Evelyne Dandry), scientist father Jean (François Marthouret) and teenage children Sophie (Marina de Van) and Nicolas (Adrien de Van) – that enjoys a comfortable, if somewhat dull, domestic existence. The just-employed Spanish maid Maria (Lucía Sánchez) half-heartedly keeps their home tidy. One evening Jean brings home a white laboratory rat as a pet for the house, of which the entire family except Hélène becomes instantly enamoured. The nameless rat appears to exert a mysterious influence: upon caressing it, each member of the family goes into a brief trance, from which he or she emerges fundamentally changed. The hitherto mousy, studious Nicolas declares his homosexuality, is seduced by Maria's Cameroo-

25 One British attitude towards *Sitcom*: 'Are we meant to be congratulating ourselves on recognising the kitsch-camp sensibility of a European John Waters fan? Or is Ozon, deep down, really expecting us to be shocked?' (Falcon, 1999: 12). One French critic describes the film as 'plutôt moins drôle que la plupart des variées sitcoms télévisuelles ... la caricature la plus éhontée ... une pure et simple mécanique vidée de toute substance' ('rather less funny than the majority of TV sitcoms ... the most shameless caricaturing ... a purely mechanical piece devoid of all substance', Bonnaud, 2001: 31).

26 The insightful *Cahiers du cinéma* article on the film is one of the rare reviews at the time of the film's release that pays tribute to the richness of its intellectual dimension, but it too criticises its style and structure as unnecessarily chaotic, describing it as a 'film bancal, désordonné, complètement kamikaze' ('wobbly, disordered, totally crash-and-burn kind of film', Lalanne, 1998: 108).

nian husband Abdu (Jules-Emmanuel Eyoum Deido), and reinvents himself as a rubber-trousered orgy king. Fresh-faced, conventional Sophie jumps out of a window, becomes paralysed from the waist down, and turns into a listless sadist, forcing her macho boyfriend David (Stéphane Rideau) to become her canine gimp. Sickened by Jean's characteristically blank refusal to react in any way to these transformations, mother Hélène too fondles the rat in desperation, after which she goes upstairs to seduce and thus 'cure' her gay son Nicolas. Finally realising, at a family therapy retreat weekend (attended by all the family except Jean), that it is indeed the rat who is to blame for the increasingly out-of-control state of the household, Hélène phones home to instruct her husband to kill the creature. He calmly complies, cooking his beloved pet in the microwave before devouring its blackened carcass. Upon mother and children's cheery return to the family home, a truly gigantic rat – the metamorphosed Jean? – leaps on Hélène and begins to rape/assault her. Sophie, having miraculously crawled out of her wheelchair, saves her mother by stabbing the monster to death, while Nicolas and David ineffectually look on. At Jean's funeral (attended by three couples: Hélène and Maria, Nicolas and Abdu, Sophie and David) a small white rat crawls over the gravestone.

For all its apparent intent to confront and unsettle its spectator, for the most part, in fact, *Sitcom* entrances and enchants from its very outset. A sharply engaging and often painfully hilarious fairy tale, presenting the simultaneous banality and intensity at the heart of so much family life within the cinematic contours of a filthy yet strangely pretty dream, it casts its spell using a vast array of truly seductive techniques. The opening credits unfold over the lush red velvet of a theatre curtain, anticipating the lush red velvet curtains and carpets of *8 femmes* and alerting the spectator to the unfettered artifice and glamour that reside at the heart of this film's sensibility. The film, this red curtain seems to announce, will clearly *not* be constrained by the everyday flatness of the 'sitcom', and will instead derive its energy precisely from the hold exercised over its characters – pitifully entrapped in blandly domestic interiors though they are – by fantasies of sensuality, passion and the perfect performance. Its two opening narrative gambits easily lure the casual viewer in too. First, the bewildering implication – we only hear its sounds – of the family's mass murder by the father (we will later discover that this bizarre starting point, from which the rest of the film unfolds as a 'flashback', is only the father Jean's dream) startles us into paying close attention, then (after the intertitle 'Three months earlier ... ') the arrival of Maria, insouciant and resolutely unservile in the manner of Jeanne Moreau's Célestine in *Journal d'une femme de chambre*, offers us a fresh outsider's eyes with which to view the central family. The film's bright colours and costumes – Hélène's leopard-skin coat (anticipating that of Catherine Deneuve in *8 femmes*, and at times identically framed as she enters the front door), Maria's orange dress and white furs, Abdu's bright-blue tracksuit tops, Nicolas's pink T-shirts, Sophie's golden hair, and thick red blood spurting here and there at key junctures – are set against the house's dazzlingly white walls and doors, and confirm Ozon as a director clearly interested, as much as Almodóvar or the French New Wave director Jacques Demy, in exploiting the signifying and affective potential of colour-based stimulation at all times. And, for the first time, Ozon demonstrates his ability to direct an ensemble cast with panache and verve, eliciting performances from the entire family and their two virtual domestics (again, a two-tiered community that will be echoed in *8 femmes*) that oscillate continually between comedy, obscenity, grotesquerie and – although this is a quality rarely mentioned in connection with this film – genuine pathos. The casting of real-life brother and sister Adrien and Marina de Van as Nicolas and Sophie is a master stroke, their naked bathtub scene all the more shocking for the actors' genuine sibling relation. And Evelyne Dandry as Hélène manages to set the template for precisely the combination of anxiety, propriety, conservatism and unwholesomeness that the film as a whole demands for its hybrid tone and social comment to function persuasively.

Most beguiling, though, is the philosophical sleight of hand set in motion by the film's central rodent actor. *Sitcom* proposes, or so it seems, its central, hypnotic, oddly cinematic animal – the rat – as a mysteriously subversive tool with which the hypocritical and oppressive structures of bourgeois family life so satirised in the first section of the film can be anarchically undermined.[27] The majority of *Sitcom*'s

27 Ozon's gleeful use of the rat as antisocial (and sickeningly comestible) cinematic symbol par excellence can be placed in a genealogy of perverse (and deeply camp) screen rats, from the rodent Bette Davis serves up to Joan Crawford in Robert Aldrich's classic *What Ever Happened to Baby Jane?* (1962) to John Waters' tribute to that unpleasant dish in the opening credits of *Desperate Living* (1975), his unbelievably overblown lesbian fairy-tale melodrama, from which Ozon will borrow liberally in *8 femmes*.

narrative is devoted to the depiction of the pursuit of a diabolical 'pact' of metamorphosis the rat appears to offer the human characters.[28] Nicolas's refusal to wash his hands after caressing the rat, despite his mother's anguished and disgusted orders to do so, signals his decision to enter into this bewildering pact. From the moment his conversation with Abdu becomes a sexual encounter – via the initial moment of intimacy provided by the blood the rat draws from Abdu's finger and Nicolas's insistent demand to see the wound – Nicolas's bedroom seems to get converted into a sort of fantastic paradise of perversion.[29] At certain times it seems to be filled by the sounds and smells of the ocean itself; at others the enormous pack of guests 'playing' within it seems to transform it into a veritable den of human rats. Sophie's encounter with the rat leads her too to attempt a plunge far outside the confines of the house's limits: rapid flight through the air would appear to be the only position she seems interested in pursuing immediately after she has caressed the rat. As for Hélène, it is only when she angrily rejects the patronising platitudes of her husband and takes the rat in her arms that she glimpses the possibility of an unprecedented kind of rapport with 'otherness' in the form of a weird new animal-son-lover. Not simply reducible to some trite Oedipal formulation, is not Hélène's decision – or, more accurately, her trance-driven propulsion – to act on her uncanny sensual experience with the rat understandable as the terrible and ecstatic pursuit of a radically unnameable relation?

Reminiscent of Pasolini's 1968 film *Theorem*, in which Terence Stamp's 'sexual angel' drives lust into the hearts of every member of the Italian family he is staying with, transforming them forever, *Sitcom* would appear to be an updated (and rather more flippant) cinematic

28 Elaborating on the manner in which the pursuit of anomalous, disruptive creatures and forces needs to be actively cultivated in everyday psychic and social life, the militantly anti-Freudian French philosophers Gilles Deleuze and Félix Guattari describe such an undertaking as the entrance into a diabolical *pact* with figures from the 'outside' – sorcerers, animals, and things defying the very categories of representation with their very 'this-ness' (*haecceitas*) (Deleuze and Guattari, 1980).

29 To the extent that Nicolas's bedroom seems to take on timeless and spaceless properties, existing only for transgressive activity and nothing else, it can be compared to the various sites of pornographic instruction and transgression in many of Sade's texts. A comparable divide between outside and inside takes place in Sade, an analogous regulation of the visitors allowed to penetrate the interior of the space of exception.

attempt to investigate the social effects of a group of characters' various communions with a bizarre new entity.[30] These communions seem to offer the path towards a radical break with the restrictive bourgeois social arena in which the family exists. But just how serious an assault *do* the various 'pacts' with the rat, and their transgressive repercussions, launch on the prevailing social and familial system at which the early part of the film pokes such fun?[31] Ozon's film – and indeed so much of his cinema – is constantly urging the spectator to look at how utterly superficial the (usually sexualised) acts that take place in the name of subversion and transformation really are. One of the most interesting things about how *Sitcom* presents its rat-inspired transgressions is its insistence on the easy absorption of each apparently transgressive act into the existing ideological fabric. Thus, despite an initial *frisson* of excitement and the sense that a serious taboo is being broken each time, having liaised with the rat, a character comes to liberate his or her desire from the shackles of convention, in every case we see the 'shocking' consequences rapidly accepted by the other characters, its subversive sting completely neutralised. Much of the film's broad comedy comes from the repetition of this phenomenon. Thus Hélène's acceptance of the fact that her son's new friends include strange semi-naked men wandering about the house requesting courgettes hammers home in satirical fashion the fact that what the film shows us is an ideological realm with astonishing capacities for accommodating activities and identities we might expect it to find unacceptably perverse. We have even reached the point, the film laughingly suggests, at which the mother–son incest taboo can be rationalised and woven into the *idées reçues* of the

---

30 The narrative similarities between the two films are striking. As Ozon himself puts it: '*Sitcom* est une sorte de *Théorème* animalier ou zoophile ... Mais c'est vraiment une idée classique: un ange exterminateur ou un étranger pénètre dans un groupe...sème la zizanie, transforme les personnages' ('*Sitcom* is a kind of animalised or bestialist *Theorem* ... But it's actually a classic idea: an exterminating angel or an outsider comes into a group ... wreaks havoc, transforms the characters', Duran, 1998). Another example from French cinema of the trope to which Ozon refers would obviously be Renoir's *Boudu sauvé des eaux* (1932).

31 Critics who take *Sitcom* seriously tend to be split between (a) those who (generally supported by Ozon's discourse around his own film) argue for an understanding of the film as subversive revelry in the proliferation of multiply queer, feminist and 'perverse' sexual identities (e.g. Chilcoat, 2007; Spoiden, 2002) and (b) those who view it as a (perhaps unwitting) critique of the dubious political use–value of such postmodern multiplicities (e.g. Asibong, 2005).

everyday: as Jean puts it in his inimitably unflappable fashion, 'Je ne pense pas que l'inceste soit la solution pour les problèmes occidentaux' ('I don't think incest will solve the West's problems'). Indeed, it is the father Jean who is the film's most farcical figure, continuing to hover, unaffected, over this miserable family melodrama, perennially platitudinous, unthreatening, tolerant and vacant. Via the unbelievably tolerant figure of Jean, *Sitcom* represents the absurd extremities of a certain 'post-ideological' liberalism that has contributed to the gradual blurring of categories of political struggle in late capitalist Western Europe: this is, perhaps, the film's most significant contribution to contemporary French cinema and culture. The Slovenian cultural theorist Slavoj Žižek observes that, in the post-1989 Western world, even as traditional paternal, patriarchal and totalitarian structures of authority seem to be dwindling, giving us the impression that freedom, happiness and democracy for all are there now for the taking, what Žižek calls an empty law continues to rule over us despotically, throwing out imaginary nuggets of enjoyment, nuggets which seem to mark out a dazzling new path to freedom – free speech, multiculturalism, queer rights – but which simply blind us to the steady progression of the same old routines of symbolic power. Žižek makes the point succinctly when he says that 'the direct injunction "Enjoy!" is a much more effective way to hinder the subject's access to enjoyment than the explicit Prohibition which sustains the space for its transgression' (Žižek, 1999: 367). In *Sitcom* Jean operates as just such a silent father or empty law, his white laboratory rat a glittering promise in animal form of freedom beyond the law. It must not be forgotten that it is Jean who brings the rat into the house with the words 'depuis longtemps je voulais un animal pour cette maison' (I've wanted an animal for this house for a long time'). The rat is his pet, it comes from his workplace, and he is the one who insists that it stay in the house. The effect the rat appears to have on his wife and children never threatens Jean's place as father within the family home, despite the spectator's reasonable expectation that, inevitably, it will. The rat, rather than operating as a subversive element, instead emerges as one that, in fact, solidifies the father-headed family framework. Nicolas and Sophie, despite their 'perverse' protestation and posturing to the contrary, never give up their unconscious attachment to a lawgiver. They locate this lawgiver, in remarkably conventional fashion, in the figure of their mild-mannered father, and they explore their relation to him via his agent the rat. At key moments in the second half of the film both Nicolas and Sophie approach Jean to ask him for some kind of approval: Nicolas asks Jean to admire his new clothes, Sophie requests her father's opinion on her physical attractiveness. What these simultaneously comical and pathetic scenes seem to be suggesting is that the less overtly the father expresses the structure of judgement his children expect of him, the more powerfully the desire for judgement operates within their unconscious. As Žižek reminds us: 'the more intensely the subject sticks to the empty form, the more traumatic the repressed content becomes' (1999: 365). Jean's refusal to prohibit becomes instead filtered through his wife's and children's psyches into a command – set in place by the rat – to *enjoy*, a command which they attempt desperately to follow but are always blocked from accomplishing, never able to attain the limitless heights of enjoyment the silent, internally operating law demands. Moreover, Žižek writes of 'the pursuit of new idiosyncratic bodily pleasures' which end up reverting to 'disinterested boredom', and notes that 'the direct intervention of pain (sadomasochistic sexual practices) [are] the only remaining path to the intense experience of pleasure' (1999: 367). Once again, the theorist's observations of contemporary society at large coincide closely with the phenomena satirically depicted by Ozon on screen through the fetish-obsessed actions of Nicolas and Sophie.

The unavoidable ambivalence at the heart of *Sitcom*'s presentation of rat-driven domestic 'rebellion' upsets any inclination we may have to posit Ozon's films as cheerily straightforward manifestoes for sexual subversion. The film's central rodent figure would appear not to catalyse truly socially disruptive forms of sexual or desire-driven transgression, then, but rather simply to channel the predictable production of static, limited and often quite reactionary 'deviant' practices and identities, easy enough for both parents to label, out on display for the calm gaze of both father and rat. At key moments in the film, Ozon's camera adopts the point of view of the rat within the cage, a point of view which allows for the creation of the impression that the rat really is the one in control, calmly regarding the family that has become its objectified plaything. It may be the one behind bars, but they are the ones functioning as the true laboratory rats – a role the pet white rat has in fact been liberated from – performing for its amusement and judgment, somehow always exposed to the seemingly panoptic power of its demonically red eyes. Under its surveillance the family – an institution which may be viewed as the ultimate breeding ground for discipline – begins to invent new (self-) regulatory regimes, its members constantly examining themselves in mirrors and spying on one other through keyholes. Ozon's *Sitcom* rat seems to destroy the film's underlying dream of revolt and renewal, encouraging its pet humans to take it up on its offer of 'new relations', but then mocking their naive gullibility as they find themselves more trapped than ever in frustrated and frustrating forms of desire. But this is clearly not the end of the story. *Sitcom*'s extraordinary array of different stages of rat–human interaction culminates, of course, in Jean's outrageous metamorphosis into the giant rat and subsequent slaying at the hands of his daughter Sophie. Some of the implications of these final developments within this film's narrative will be considered at greater length in Chapters 3 and 4. What is important to retain, for the moment, is that *Sitcom* brings home most comprehensively the growing conviction developed in the course of viewing the shorts: sexual transgression and experimentation with identity are both key to Ozon's vision of cinema, desire and perhaps existence itself. They are not, in and of themselves, however, to be viewed as any kind of vehicle for serious social change. For that, far more radical forms of onscreen metamorphosis may be required.

References

Asibong, Andrew (2005) 'Meat, murder, metamorphosis: the transformational ethics of François Ozon', *French Studies*, 59(2): 203–15.

Bingham, Adam (2003) 'Identity and love: the not-so-discreet charm of François Ozon', *Kinoeye*, (13).

Bonnaud, Frédéric (2001) *Les Inrockuptibles*, 324: 30–1.

Chilcoat, Michelle (2007) 'Queering the family in François Ozon's *Sitcom*', in R. Griffiths (ed.), *Queer Cinema in Europe*, Bristol, Intellect Books.

Deleuze, Gilles and Guattari, Félix (1980) *Mille Plateaux: Capitalisme et Schizophrénie II*, Paris, Minuit.

Doustaly, Thomas (1999) 'Interview transgenre', *Têtu*, 37.

Duralde, Alonso (2006) 'Time after time', *Advocate*, 15 August.

Duran, Claude (1998) interview with François Ozon, *Têtu*, 24.

Falcon, Richard (1999) 'Reality is too shocking', *Sight & Sound* 9(1): 10–13.

ffrench, Patrick (2005) 'The memory of the image in Chris Marker's *La Jetée*', *French Studies*, 59(1): 31–7.

Ince, Kate (2008) 'François Ozon', in Ince, Kate (ed.), *Auteurship from Assayas to Ozon: Five Directors*, Manchester, Manchester University Press.

Johnston, Cristina (2002) 'Representations of homosexuality in 1990s mainstream French cinema', *Studies in French Cinema*, 2(1): 23–31.

Lacan, Jacques (1975) *Le Séminaire, Livre XX: Encore, 1972–1973*, Paris, Seuil.

Lalanne, Jean-Marc (1998) 'La Place du père et celle du rat', *Cahiers du cinéma*, 524: 107–8.

Mulvey, Laura (2006) *Death 24x a Second: Stillness and the Moving Image*, London, Reaktion.

Schiller, Britt-Marie 'On the threshold of the creative imagination: *Swimming Pool* (2003)', *International Journal of Psychoanalysis*, 86: 557–66.

Spoiden, Stéphane (2002) 'No man's land: genres en question dans *Sitcom, Romance* et *Baise-moi*', *L'Esprit Créateur*, 42(1): 96–106.

Žižek, Slavoj (1999) *The Ticklish Subject: The Absent Centre of Political Ontology*, London/New York, Verso.

Internet sources

www.francois-ozon.com, accessed July 2007.

1 Fluid identities: Paul (François Delaive) and Martial (Martial Jacques) take a shower in the short family melodrama *La Petite Mort* (1994)

2 Surviving Daddy: an imaginary snap-shot of the family, resurrected and smiling, after its hallucinated massacre by Papa (*Sitcom*, 1998)

3 The rat as phallus-fetish: pre-transformation Nicolas (Adrien de Van) reaches out for 'amour, dialogue, tendresse' in *Sitcom* (1998)

4 Easy prey: mother and baby (Sasha Hails and Samantha, foreground), about to be visited by Tatiana (Marina de Van, background) in *Regarde la mer* (1997)

5 Leopold (Bernard Giraudeau) presides over Anna (Ludivine Sagnier), Franz (Malik Zidi) and Vera (Anna Thomson) in *Gouttes d' eau sur pierres brûlantes* (1999)

6 Master of the house Leopold (Bernard Giraudeau) shows little Franz (Malik Zidi) his place in *Gouttes d' eau sur pierres brûlantes* (1999)

7 The stars and actresses of *8 femmes* (2001) bathe in ephemeral equality for a publicity still

8 A singing wound: the broken Madame Chanel (Firmine Richard) sings 'Pour ne pas vivre seul' alone in her kitchen in *8 femmes* (2001)

9 Marie (Charlotte Rampling) and the masturbatory fantasy of plenitude in *Sous le sable* (2000)

10 A rare moment of 'natural' pleasure: Sarah (Charlotte Rampling) feels the sun on her face in *Swimming Pool* (2003)

11 'Il n'y a pas de rapport sexuel', Part 1: Marion (Valeria Bruni-Tedeschi) and Gilles (Stéphane Freiss) at the start of their wedding night in *5x2* (2004)

12 'Il n'y a pas de rapport sexuel', Part 2: Romain (Melvil Poupaud) excluded, post-*coitus*, from the trio in *Le Temps qui reste* (2005)

2

Master and servant: society, spectacle and sadomasochistic cinema

François Ozon's films frequently employ household servants among their cast of characters. In Ozon's cinema, these domestic figures seem designed not merely to illustrate the bourgeois status of the other protagonists, but rather as crucial players in their own right, catalysts for the main action in the narrative, the location of the very possibility for the subversion of the social world contained within the films. In common with Buñuel's maid Célestine (*Le Journal d'une femme de chambre*, France, 1964), Losey's valet Barrett (*The Servant*, UK, 1963), and Fassbinder's dogsbody Marlene (*The Bitter Tears of Petra von Kant*, West Germany, 1972), Ozon's cinematic servants frequently display a simultaneously playful and belligerent capacity for resistance and transformation, the culmination of which is usually a rapid overtaking of their confused and stagnating employers and an apparent rise to the heights of dominance – domestic, sexual, economic, or all three. As early as *Victor*, Ozon was rehearsing his master–servant role-reversal domestic scenario of predilection, and *Sitcom* further developed the theme in characteristically comic–pornographic style. (Filing her nails and dancing in the living room to techno in her first week of domestic employment, and aggressively masturbating the fiancé of the household in her first month, by *Sitcom*'s finale the maid Maria appears to have become her mistress Hélène's authoritative lesbian partner.) By the time Emmanuelle Béart, as the maid Louise in *8 femmes* (2001), belligerently, contemptuously and seductively sings the song 'Pile ou face' ('Heads or Tails') to the befuddled middle-class spinster aunt Augustine (Isabelle Huppert), going on to wear the mistress Gaby (Catherine Deneuve)'s furs while making explicit sexual overtures to her and openly throwing cigarette ash on the floor, we have become familiar with this particular table-turning Ozonian fantasy. The often-repeated dynamic is hardly a cinematic theorisation of proletarian revolution, of course. Ozon's rebelling servants seem much of the time to remain essentially postmodern, playful and erotic, Béart and Firmine Richard in *8 femmes* coming across as light-hearted lesbian pastiches of the pre-existing cinematic models of Buñuel's aforementioned Célestine and Douglas Sirk's saintly black housekeeper Annie in *Imitation of Life* (1958).[1] There is no Marxist-Leninist analysis of the master–servant dynamic spouted by theory-literate characters in the manner of, say, Godard or Pasolini, nor are there even the explicitly socio-historical codas offered by apparently more compromising directors such as Buñuel and Sirk, who are still keen to make sure their master-servant prototypes exist within a politically contextualised arena.[2] When the Ozonian servant rebels, she does so not in the spirit of 1917 (or even 1968), but instead in one that might be instead described as resolutely 'post-1989', a spirit characterised not by organised uprising and the establishment of coherent collectives, but rather by individual transgression and thrill-seeking border-crossing. The servants remain deeply fetish driven, unapologetically phantasmatic figures, the masturbatory material of an essentially sadomasochistic imaginary revelling in the idea of simultaneously powerful and debased slave girls in stiletto heels. Is Ozon's apparent cinematic revelry in the representation of unequal power dynamics an ultimately apolitical one, then? Do his films irresponsibly conflate embedded social inequalities with erotically ritualised ones? How seriously, for example, should we attempt to read the mistress–gimp relationship between Sophie and David in *Sitcom*, the collar and

1 Ozon is not the first director to take the white mistress–black housekeeper relation inaugurated by Scarlett and Mammy in *Gone with the Wind* (1939) into new (frequently psycho-sexual) terrain, then. With the Lora–Annie relation in *Imitation of Life* Sirk underlines the unspoken emotional dependencies of its perverse dynamic, while both Fassbinder (with surrealistic melodrama in *Whity*, 1970) and John Waters (with pornographic hilarity in *Desperate Living*, 1977) emphasise its highly sexualised subtext.

2 In his remake of *Journal d'une femme de chambre* Buñuel adds the unforgettable final sequence in which a baying French fascist crowd cries 'A bas les métèques!' ('Down with the foreign scum!') as the chambermaid of the title looks on, while in his own remake of *Imitation of Life* Sirk creates an equally overwhelming final sequence: the housekeeper Annie's African-American funeral, alerting the spectator to the sheer speechless invisibility of blackness in the rest of the film.

chain to which the 'ogre' keeps Luc attached before he sodomises him in *Les Amants criminels*, the striking mention of the Marquis de Sade's castle in *Swimming Pool* or the leather-clad denizens of the gay backroom in *Le Temps qui reste*? One approach we might adopt would be to consider to what extent Ozon's emphasis on artificial, chosen and highly ritualised processes of debasement allows his films to explore potential ways in which more wide-reaching hierarchies and stratifications might, at least theoretically, become unmoored, via exaggerated 'overrepresentation', from their fixed positions.[3] Once we begin exploring Ozonian power dynamics in this way, however, we begin to uncover a genuine tension between, on the one hand, flexible, fluid, ludic forms of reversible subjugation and, on the other, more entrenched, rigid and overwhelming forms of power that crush those in its path regardless of their individual wiles. Ozon's cinematic masters and servants play their games in a landscape where they may choose certain sadomasochistic postures, yes, but where far larger, machine-like forces of psychic and social domination devour and consume subjects according to a quite implacable logic.

The complexities of the ambiguous, two-tiered power dynamics to be found among Ozon's characters in films between 1997 and 2001 emerge from a brief preliminary revisiting of the figures of Maria and Abdu in the 1998 comedy *Sitcom*. The Spanish maid and her Cameroonian gym teacher husband are exceptional figures in the film, since they are simultaneously affected and strangely unaffected by the rat's magical powers: interestingly, they hover between their original personalities and the new, pseudo-transgressive ones ushered in by interaction with the rat. Neither led into an unconscious, all-consuming belief in the rat as transformational agent, as son Nicolas, daughter Sophie and mother Hélène seem to be, nor metamorphosed into a horrific monstrosity like the father Jean, Abdu and Maria tend, throughout the film, to steer a path between these extremes. Abdu seduces Nicolas, certainly, but undergoes no radical change of personality that we are aware of; Maria seduces Sophie's fiancé David but, again, appears to retain control and a certain flippancy vis-à-vis her act.

3 The French novelist and playwright Jean Genet, for example, revealed various (sexualised) techniques of parody and self-conscious role-playing among his various subaltern characters (consider the eponymous maids and Blacks of the plays *Les Bonnes* (1949) and *Les Nègres* (1958) respectively) precisely to undermine the essentialism of the hierarchical structures in place.

Furthermore, neither part of the family nor quite outside it, neither French nor quite foreign, neither heterosexual nor quite gay, neither part of the ruling class nor quite oppressed, Maria and Abdu seem merrily to exemplify the postmodern, post-political, 'queer' subject. However, if we examine the function of the duo within the film a little more closely, we realise that their apparently powerful manipulation of their bourgeois employers, expressed via this putative flexibility, is in fact secondary to the far more hard-hitting, symbolic violence suffered by these servant figures throughout the film. This greater violence lies in the film's subtle conflation – via its narrative structure, its exposition of casually racist dialogue and its various aesthetic choices – of the servants themselves with a rat-like status. Maria's arrival in the family home coincides, for example, with that of the rat. For a short time at the start of the film, then, the audience expects *her* to be the catalyst that will set in motion whatever intrigue the filmmaker clearly has in store for us. When Abdu arrives on Maria's arm for dinner the same night, the palpable visual shock Ozon engineers for both his spectator (who, it seems, is expected to sit up in surprise at the sudden appearance in this white house of a very dark-skinned black man in incongruous evening dress) and characters (particularly Hélène, who visibly shudders) is directly analogous with the physically expressed shock displayed by Hélène when Jean brings home his rat. The rat itself seems aware of Abdu and Maria as being somehow different from the rest of the family: it sits up in Maria's hair rather than be cradled in her arms and, as for Abdu, it bites him each time he touches it, drawing blood at each meeting (Abdu is the only character who, as it were, goes back for more). The film shows Abdu and Maria as being constantly recognised and simultaneously not recognised by both family and rat as 'normal' human subjects. Hélène will refer to Abdu with her psychoanalyst as 'le mari noir de ma bonne' ('my maid's black husband') but will also invite him to join her for tea and sympathy on the sofa. Maria's breasts will be welcomed as desirable sexual objects by an excited David, but he will fling her body away in disgust when Sophie unexpectedly turns up. Maria and Abdu are accepted into the family home on exactly the same terms as the rat: as pet-like entities to perform for the family at the appropriate time and place. All three figures visibly hover on the film's landscape between being, on the one hand, social creatures, fully integrated members of the central family, and, on the other, partially or wholly fetishised carriers of alternating fascination and disgust. Since *Sitcom* is, after all, a comedy – albeit an extremely black one – the spectator tends only to see the funny side of these situations. And yet, the viewer willing to read the film against the grain, to consider images seemingly served up by the resolutely non-engaged Ozon as mere post-ideological spectacle, may edge towards the discovery of the following well-concealed paradox: at least two levels of power exist within the film's discourse. At a comic, titillating and fundamentally superficial level of the film's action, Maria and Abdu do indeed hold a powerfully 'sadistic' sway over the family. At a less overt and generally silenced register of the film, however, the spectator glimpses Maria and Abdu as vermin, slaves even more masochistically supine within Jean's family machine than Hélène and the children. The political implications of this multi-layered power dynamic are never really explored in Ozon's cinema in the way that a clear-headed social theoretician-cum-filmmaker like the Fassbinder of *Fear Eats the Soul* (1973) would have gone about it: Ozon seems much of the time almost oblivious to the sheer ethico-political urgency of some of the scenarios by which his films are so evidently fascinated. The dynamic is repeated again and again, however – too often *not* to be carefully and critically picked apart by the spectator attentive to the interplay of such politically inflected signs on film.

Flirting with Medusa: *Regarde la mer* (1997)

Ozon filmed the curiously intermediate-length (it runs at 52 minutes) *Regarde la mer*, the film that may well prove to be his indisputable masterpiece, over two weeks in 1997. It was released in France in the December of that year. A summer-holiday seaside piece, like the jolly short *Une Robe d'été* that immediately precedes it, the film could not be further removed from the light-hearted exploratory tone that characterised that earlier film, and is instead Ozon's most shockingly sadistic piece to date, a fact all the more disturbing for the relentless good taste and restraint the film seems at first to exude, a good taste embodied in the exceedingly polite person of Sasha Hails (who was justifiably rewarded with the Best Actress prize at the Pantin Film Festival for her pains). Transforming quite suddenly, according to Ozon, from a project about a father and son on an island entitled *Sous le sable*, into a female two-hander about the cruel, bizarre and ultimately unspeakably violent relations between a charming young mother and a truculent woman backpacker, it was apparently Ozon's 'coup de foudre' (in his words) for a pierced, shaven-headed, beer-swilling female traveller glimpsed by chance on a boat that set the new film in motion (see *Regarde la mer* French DVD audio commentary).

Sasha (Sasha Hails), a pretty young Englishwoman, is alone, save for her 10-month-old baby daughter Siofra (played by Hails's real-life daughter Samantha), one summer in her holiday home on the French Atlantic island of Yeu. Her French husband is away in Paris on business. Sasha spends her solitary days chatting to the pre-articulate Siofra, sitting on the beach and reading. One day the tranquillity is disturbed by a young Frenchwoman, Tatiana (Marina de Van), who turns up at Sasha's doorstep and asks if she might – or, rather, states that she will – put up her tent in Sasha's garden for a few days. Overwhelmed (but also visibly entranced) by Tatiana's rough, monosyllabic forcefulness, Sasha politely concedes. Despite Tatiana's manner (an indifference bordering on sociopathic rudeness), Sasha makes increasingly friendly attempts to win the company and approval of her visitor, inviting her into the house for dinner (during which Tatiana both interrogates and insults her hospitality), allowing her to use the bathroom (during which Tatiana smokes marijuana and masturbates in the bath and, more upsettingly, dips Sasha's toothbrush into the toilet bowl into which she has just defecated), and leaving Siofra in her company (during which Tatiana encourages the baby to play with her tongue piercings). Tatiana appears to have cast a spell over Sasha, who watches the sullen young backpacker in her glowing red tent from her window at night, all the while rubbing a chair between her legs. The spell seems to be causing Sasha to lose all powers of judgement and propriety: one day when the two women and the baby are together at the beach Tatiana points out gay men having sex in the woods, before abruptly leaving mother and baby to amuse themselves. Immediately, Sasha leaves the baby on the hot beach and wanders into the woods, where she allows a strange man to perform cunnilingus on her. Meanwhile, Tatiana goes wandering in the local graveyard, fingering cracks in ancient and decaying graves with fascination. The narrative builds towards its climax. Despite having found (through a compulsive desire to snoop) a terrifying notebook in Tatiana's tent, containing demented drawing, scrawling and the name 'Caroline' written hundreds of times, Sasha invites Tatiana in for dinner once more, a dinner during which the terrifying backpacker quizzes her about her childbirth experience, asking to what extent her vagina tore, before announcing that she herself had her own baby aborted. Visibly shaken, Sasha nevertheless asks Tatiana to stay the night – her husband is due back the next day. During the night, Tatiana comes to watch the naked mother and baby as they sleep, before weeping and silently pulling off her own clothes. The next day Sasha's husband Paul (Paul Raoux) returns. Finding nobody at home, he looks inside the mysterious red tent in the garden, where he discovers Sasha's dead body bound with several coils of rope, a bag over her head, and her vagina sewn up. The last scene of the film shows Tatiana sailing from the island on a boat, a screaming Siofra cradled in her arms. The ocean shimmers, a sublime, sun-soaked azure.

At one level, *Regarde la mer* can be viewed as a supremely elegant comedy of manners, almost in the tradition of Buñuel, picking apart the neuroses and compulsions of a repressed bourgeois housewife with a playful savagery. It is, on the surface, a tale of social order turned upside down, Sasha's order and privilege (with an upper-class English accent to boot!) finding itself slowly but surely eroded – through her own boredom and appetite for self-destruction – by the dominant invading force of Tatiana, an apparently homeless, marginal, working-class drifter.[4] The film mercilessly analyses how, at every step, it is Sasha's inherent masochism that characterises her relation with Tatiana, a masochism that overrides and ultimately dwarfs the putative class and economic differences that exist between the two women. An eroticised cruelty dominates every aspect of their interaction. From the moment Tatiana arrives at her door, Sasha appears to take a certain pleasure in the lack of respect shown to her, with every display of contempt offering the stranger – against all logic or good sense – more and more of herself, her home and her baby for desecration. When Tatiana unapologetically barges into the bathroom where Sasha is bathing with Siofra Sasha is visibly uncomfortable, and yet accepts the situation, going out of her way to allow further

4 Tatiana might be considered as a filmic descendant of the Sandrine Bonnaire character in Agnès Varda's *Sans toit ni loi* (1985), a film widely considered to be a classic of French feminist cinema. Interestingly, Ozon (frequently labelled a misogynist director by some critics) grants far more agency (albeit of a psychotic kind) to his homeless female drifter than Varda does hers.

violations to take place. When Tatiana violently squirts white lotion onto Siofra's stomach in a shockingly semen-like torrent, simultaneously massaging Sasha's neck in an uncomfortably throttle-like motion, Sasha submits to what is clearly, for her, a sensuous experience. The final dinner interrogation is filmed as an exercise in the excesses of perversely cruel dialogue: a series of brutally close-up shot-reverse shots of the two women, one forcing the other to give up and articulate the most private experience of her recent years, the 'victim' (as played by the blushing Hails) displaying embarrassment, discomfort, anger and pleasure all at once, the 'torturer' (as played by the simultaneously stony and impish de Van) revealing nothing, only an inhuman drive to *know*.

The film is prevented, though, from being an essentially light-hearted treatise on bourgeois masochism and its power to disrupt the everyday workings of class domination by a number of serious stumbling blocks, all of which render it difficult to revel in the subversive potential of any kind of sadomasochistic 'flexibility'. First, Sasha's (complicit) descent into victimhood may indeed be interesting when considered from a perspective solely interested in her standing as the middle-class English wife of a powerful French businessman, but other factors render her eventual butchery impossible to consider as a subversion of the prevailing social order depicted on-screen. Her evident solitude – refracted through the strongly gendered situation of being a woman alone with only a baby for company – renders her immeasurably vulnerable to abuse. Sasha's attempts to establish relations (of any kind) with Tatiana frequently appear as desperate stabs at human intimacy, at any price. Her awkward *récit* at the first dinner she prepares for Tatiana, in which she (or rather, Hails: the tale is, according to Ozon's commentary on the DVD, both improvised and genuine) recounts touchingly unfunny high jinks in Morocco as a younger woman, is heartbreaking in the warmth and spontaneity of its delivery, especially given its blankly icy reception by Tatiana. As is the case with the various family members of *Sitcom* in their attempts to establish 'amour, dialogue, tendresse' with the rat, Sasha's vain desire to reach out to the fantastically unpromising Tatiana separates her transgression immeasurably from the class-obsessed masochistic shenanigans of, say, the perverse *bourgeoise* Séverine, as played by Catherine Deneuve, in Buñuel's satire *Belle de jour* (1966). Sasha – foreign, open, over-feminised and sincere – is cut out for a quite inflexible subject-positioning as victim quite unrelated to a class-related game of temporary role-reversal.

Furthermore, the non-playful violence of Sasha's predestined butchery is reinforced by the quite shockingly real manner in which both Ozon, in his capacity as director, and Marina de Van, in her capacity as actress and apparent confidante of Ozon, speak in their DVD commentary of having knowingly manipulated the actress Sasha Hails. Ozon speaks elsewhere of a desire, dating from his first meeting with Hails before the filming of *Une Rose entre nous*, to find a way to do the actress a certain harm on film: 'Déjà l'envie de la maltraiter et de la sadiser apparaissait' ('Already my desire to treat her badly and to be sadistic towards her was starting to emerge', Ozon official website, 'Interviews sur les Courts-Métrages'). By the time of *Regarde la mer* this desire seems to have grown to a point where his cinematic abuse of the character conflates imperceptibly with his personal abuse of the actress. Sharing the truly horrific nature of the film with de Van but not with Hails, Ozon ends up effectively capturing both Hails and her baby on film in an activity over which neither has any control.[5] Ozon speaks merrily of the importance of keeping Hails ignorant of the fact that her character's toothbrush has been dipped in shit. De Van talks in amusement of springing the entire interrogation about childbirth, vaginal damage, excrement and infection on her unprepared and flabbergasted co-star, in the full knowledge that Hails had not only recently given birth, but was imminently due to do so again. And together Ozon and de Van laugh about the fact that Hails was terrified that de Van might drop Hails's baby in the sea in the film's final shot. Together, Ozon and de Van – themselves both film directors, de Van coming to international prominence with her debut feature about self-harm *Dans ma peau* (2002) – strengthen the sadistic power of the character Sasha's victimisation through a genuine, unfeigned and non-playful obliteration of Hails's agency as actress.[6]

---

5 Ozon seems above all entertained by the fact that Hails had imagined the film's climax to be a lesbian encounter between the two women rather than the actual denouement in which her character ends up 'se faire trucider' ('getting herself cut to pieces', DVD commentary).

6 Cinema history is, of course, littered with examples of male directors boasting of their psychological bullying of their female leads in the aim of eliciting the right degree of on-screen victimhood from her (consider Stanley Kubrick and Shelley Duvall on the set of *The Shining* (1980) or Lars von Trier and Björk on *Dancer in the Dark* (2001)).

Regarde la mer flirts with the idea of sadomasochistic interaction being an essentially ludic, erotic and socially destabilising practice, then, but ultimately the overwhelming nature of the film's sadism is altogether more inflexible. Tatiana is no mask-wearing maid or leather-clad dominatrix with revolution on her mind but is, rather, an agent of total destruction, a horror-machine pure and simple. The very first shot we have of Tatiana – a low-angle long shot of her perched at the top of a cliff like an eagle, her backpack cemented to her like a dead baby, seen by the attentive Siofra but not by the oblivious Sasha – frames her as a sort of nemesis, utterly terrifying in her potential to swoop and devour. Later shots of her reinforce with relentless force this inhuman, monstrous dimension. During the first dinner sequence, de Van and Hails are filmed in a fantastically contrasting manner: while Hails is bathed in a basically 'realistic' light, de Van's white, luminous face is surrounded by utter blackness, and shines out of the dark with a disturbingly supernatural effect.[7] As Tatiana wanders down endless supermarket aisles of raw meat (juxtaposed with rows of nappies), the viewer begins to see her as a potential butcher from another dimension, a truly Sadeian (rather than simply 'sadistic') figure, whose later associations with the forced ingestion of faeces, and of course, the mutilation of a vagina by needle and thread, hammer home the comparison with unapologetic force.[8] A true precursor to *Sitcom*'s magical rat, like Michel Piccoli's devilish Husson in Buñuel's *Belle de jour*, she contaminates her prey with the desire for fruitless transgression, before swallowing the hapless transgressor with a truly cataclysmic force.[9] There is no negotiation possible within this particular framework of sadistic practice, no chance of a reconfiguration of roles and desires according to the manifestoes of the more optimistic

7 The sequence is reminiscent of both Bergman's *Persona* (1966) and Altman's *3 Women* (1977) in its excessive use of the shot-reverse-shot technique to film a long, coercive dialogue between two women, one of whom starts to emerge as an otherworldly figure.

8 Sade's epic *120 journées de Sodome* (1785), as well as Pasolini's notorious film version *Salò* (1976) features torturers who force their victims to eat excrement, while Sade's later *Philosophie dans le boudoir* (1795) culminates in a teenage daughter's sewing up of her mother's vagina.

9 Tatiana is 'un fantôme qui emprunte l'enveloppe rassurante d'un vampire de film d'horreur' ('a ghost who takes on the reassuring mantle of a horror film vampire', Jousse, 1997: 67).

contemporary cultural theorists of gender trouble and identity play.[10] The ultimately weaker partner, Sasha, will be annihilated in the most violent fashion imaginable. The stronger partner, Tatiana, will operate from a zone of absolute power, and will be lifted out of the realms of the human through her immersion in that zone. Traits considered as 'feminine' will be punished with a ruthless savagery; the female body itself will be mutilated beyond recognition; the female baby will be carried away to a fate potentially too obscene to be represented. And Paul, the all-but-invisible husband and father who returns to survey the scene of carnage at the film's climax, Paul, whose distance and silent authority has fixed Sasha into her designated position as victim from the start, and on whose land the whole disgusting interaction takes place, will emerge unscathed.

Fairy-tale therapy: *Les Amants criminels* (1998)

The critical success of *Regarde la mer* allowed Ozon to make his first feature, *Sitcom*, but it was not until his second feature *Les Amants criminels*, released in France in August 1999, that he returned to that more serious and knowingly overwrought register within which he could explore the vagaries of a violently socialised sadomasochism with a sense of real drama.[11] *Les Amants criminels*, though, was largely hated by public and critics alike.[12] Its unabashed preoccupation with the ethics and aesthetics of murder, cannibalism and sodomy was

10 *Gender Trouble: Feminism and the Subversion of Identity* (1990), the American philosopher Judith Butler's hugely successful enquiry into the politics of identity performance and reconfiguration, would be an obvious example of postmodernist theory seeking to grant the power of agency and transformation to knowingly experimenting sexual subjects.

11 In France, the article on the film in *Cahiers du cinéma* gets straight to the heart of Ozon's achievement in stating that 'c'est le désir qui conduit Ozon dans son geste de cinéma et seulement le désir, loin des fausses transgressions bourgeoises et conventionelles' ('it's desire that leads Ozon towards his cinematic gesture, and desire alone, far from the falseness of bourgeois and conventional transgressions', Jousse, 1997: 67), while in the UK the *Time Out* review claims that 'every cut signals a startling, disquieting talent'.

12 According to the influential cultural magazine *Les Inrockuptibles*, 'ce fut un carnage: éreintement unanime de la part de la presse et désastre commercial' ('it was a bloodbath: a unanimous critical slating from the press and a commercial disaster', Bonnaud, 2001: 30).

doubtless indigestible, and yet, along with *Regarde la mer*, the film offers the most simultaneously thoughtful, innovative and exciting exploration of the nuances and pitfalls of 'power play' Ozon has been able to offer to date. Alice (Natacha Régnier), a teenage girl in an unnamed French province, persuades Luc (Jérémie Renier), her devoted but impotent boyfriend, to kill Saïd (Salim Kechiouche), a hyper-masculine and athletic classmate, whom she (falsely) accuses of having orchestrated her gang rape in the basement of the housing estate where he lives. Reluctantly complying with Alice's wishes, Luc stabs Saïd to death one night in the gym shower room where Alice has summoned her alleged aggressor for a sexual rendezvous. Stealing Luc's father's car, the querulous couple head into the woods, where they bury Saïd's body, silently watched by an unknown figure. They cannot find their way out of the woods, however, since their tracks have been covered over by enormous footprints. Stealing food from an isolated cottage, the pair are trapped inside by its owner, a huge bearded huntsman (Miki Manojlovic), who throws them into a rat-infested pit in which the dug up and partially mutilated corpse of Saïd also lies rotting. Uninterested in the increasingly demented Alice, the forest 'ogre' instead seizes only her incriminating diary, before hauling Luc out of the pit in order to bathe him, put him on a lead, fatten him with boiled rabbit (and, it is suggested, with Saïd's boiled flesh), successfully masturbate him, sodomise him and perhaps eventually eat him. Stealing the ogre's rifle as he slumbers, but refusing to murder his giant 'lover', Luc flees with Alice back into the woods, at last finding an idyllic watery glade where they begin to have penetrative sex for the first time. The law is on their trail, however: Alice is shot dead as she attempts to turn the rifle on the police, and Luc, caught in a stray rabbit trap and resigned to his punishment, is thrown into a police van. Sobbing with fury as he watches the arrested ogre outside the van being kicked to the ground by the gang of *gendarmes*, he eventually stops to gaze, with enraged lucidity, at the camera.[13]

Two versions of the film exist: the 1998 original, which more or

13 Luc's final gaze at the camera is a quite remarkable moment of cinema, compared by Mark Hain to 'the chilling look of Norman Bates (Anthony Perkins) at the end of *Psycho*, a look that conveys the character's active *thinking* as powerfully as his seeing' (2007: 285). Hain goes on to establish a number of parallels between the film and *Psycho* (a shower murder, the ogre's cabin as a Bates Motel equivalent and, of course, the plethora of dead animals).

less begins with Saïd's murder, the early, clandestine details of Alice's obsession with Saïd only emerging in the second half of the film as the ogre reads her diary, and the reworked 2001 version which, somewhat less interestingly, offers us the story in totally chronological order, with no flashbacks. Like *Regarde la mer* before it and the Fassbinder adaptation *Gouttes d'eau sur pierres brûlantes* that would immediately follow it, *Les Amants criminels* is haunted by Ozon's apparent preoccupation during this period with a certain 'wrong turn' taken by human fantasy, with the jarring disjunction between sadomasochistic game-playing (with all its smug assumptions about reversibility, reconfiguration and productive transgression) and the all-engulfing sadistic machine that invariably swallows its true, non-negotiable victims. For the greater part of the film, both Alice and Luc labour under the delusion that their various adventures – sexual transgressions, rape fantasies, murder realities – all revolving around the fetishised, exoticised and ultimately dehumanised (by characters and Ozon alike) figure of the ethnic 'other' – Saïd – lie within their controlled, autonomous desire. Saïd – like the rat of *Sitcom* – is clearly linked in the white teenage couple's consciousnesses to transgression, a connection rendered explicit in an early scene of the film in which Alice gleefully recites Rimbaud's lines 'Un crime – vite!' as she draws the contours of Saïd's head. Saïd comes to represent for Alice a means by which she can conceive of two extreme, 'impossible' versions of her own sexuality: utterly passive, as she fantasises about being raped by him, and totally active, as she tells him aggressively: 'C'est moi qui te niquerai, petit con!' ('I'm the one who'll fuck you, you little asshole!'). Through the contemplation of this desired but despised personage, Alice feels that anything is possible. No less troublingly, Luc fixates on Saïd as the means through which he thinks he can manage his own frustrated desire. As he watches the bigger, stronger boy boxing or urinating or 'bonding' with an equally macho buddy, we see Luc's face fill with worried fascination: in Saïd's 'natural', spontaneous, uncomplicatedly masculine physicality, all Luc's own unspoken complexes around his all too 'cultural' shyness, impotence, and multilayered sexuality, find a bodily focus of simultaneous resentment and desire. Alice and Luc's sadistic objectification of Saïd takes place largely through the gaze with which they apprehend him. Saïd appears, at least on the surface, to be at least as equipped to objectify Luc and Alice as they are to objectify him, to be a player against them in an equal battle, a contestant in an equitably sadomasochistic game. After all, he treats Alice to an assortment of banal sexual overtures, and gently mocks Luc for his purported lack of sexual prowess. And yet in the sections of the film where he is still alive, Ozon's camera is staunchly on the side of his white protagonists' desire, making of Saïd the only real object. In the classroom where Alice feverishly sketches him, she is positioned behind him, able to behold him constantly and at her leisure, while he must turn around in his seat in order to look at her. Watching Saïd in the boxing ring, at the urinal and in the shower alike, the viewer shares with Luc and Alice the privilege of gazing at this dark body from behind, from the side and from the (full) front. As Saïd, the actor Salim Kechiouche becomes instigated as the film's truly sexual specimen, a thoroughly eroticised sight to behold with wonder, an object-function Jérémie Renier and Natacha Regnier as Luc and Alice tend not to perform, even when shown naked.[14] And while Ozon apparently considered filming the murder scene from Saïd's perspective, he quickly rejected this idea: 'C'était trop violent pour une scène qui se place au début du film. Donc je me suis dit: "Prenons le côté fait divers justement. On va se positionner loin"' ('It was too violent for a scene placed at the start of the film. So I said to myself, "Let's really go for the news story angle, then. We'll take up our position at a distance"', Guillomeau and Thoret, 1999). Saïd is sealed into his fate as 'thing', then, both within the film's diegesis and by the camera itself. Alice's lengthy and detailed lie regarding her alleged gang rape by Saïd's *banlieue* band of friends, meanwhile, encases Saïd into the sexualised fantasy image of young men of Arabic descent propagated by French media headlines and hardcore pornography alike, heavily dependent as both so desperately are on the racialised clichés and stereotypes of the ghetto youth and his depraved nocturnal activities.

The crucial 'avenging angel' figure of the ogre is the only entity, it would appear, capable of destabilising the sadistic logic of the victim–executioner positioning set up so firmly by the triad of Alice, Luc and Ozon's camera. He achieves this not through an appeal to the reversibility of sadomasochistic play, but via his startling theory and practice of non-negotiable bondage, together with the revelation of an ineluctable transformation that these unspeakably new forms of

14 Consider Alice and Luc's own shower after the murder scene, for example: the camera remains fixed on their heads and upper bodies, certainly not drinking in the sight of their nudity as it did with Saïd just a few minutes earlier.

punishment will bring in their wake. In presenting Alice and Luc with the corpse of Saïd, rotting, mutilated and staring, the body they thought they could simply dispose of once its function as receptacle of violent desire had been exhausted, he forces them to look at their disavowed desire in returned, obscene, un-integrated form.[15] Luc alone (for Alice is excluded from this journey, so deeply trapped is she in a world of spectacle and desire) will be transformed by his encounter with this new master, coming to occupy a position outside the neurotic cycles in which he was previously embroiled. For the ogre, he can become a slave, and be made to wear a chain and collar; he can become a rabbit ('mon petit lapin'), ripe for fattening up and death by consumption; he can become a sex toy, to be played with at whim. Luc can even become Saïd himself: in Alice's feverish yet utterly *correct* masturbatory dream-scape (to which, at one point in the film, we as spectators are privy) the two boys are literally interchangeable. It is no longer just Saïd who can be placed under a regime of intense surveillance, no longer just Saïd who can be ruthlessly penetrated, no longer just Saïd who can be unflinchingly eaten. Luc's body too can be rendered a deathly object purely through the manner in which the life within it is handled and managed. If Luc gazes at the beaten ogre in the film's final frames with something approaching love, it is surely because the latter has taught him a lesson most people can only find within annihilation itself.

Whatever the critics and audiences made of *Les Amants criminels*, it is crucial to acknowledge it as a key feature in Ozon's trajectory. Ozon proves himself for the second time a director able not only to pilfer earlier cinematic works with taste and intelligence, but to re-envision their values within a provocatively postmodern framework that trans-figures them. Here, it is Charles Laughton's terrifying fable *Night of the Hunter* (1955) that is nodded to with most frequency: Luc and Alice become sexualised, fallen versions of the American babes on the run from the wicked beast, but find no little old granny figure to protect them. Instead, Ozon conflates the Robert Mitchum–monster and the Lillian Gish–earth mother within a single figure: an ogre who is as ethically helpful as he is sexually predatory.[16] The erotics of a fantasised

15 They are forced, as Ozon puts it, 'de bouffer d'une certaine manière [leur] merde' ('to eat their own shit, in a way', Guillomeau and Thoret, 1999).
16 Clearly Arthur Penn's *Bonnie and Clyde* (1967) serves as another important intertext for the film, Clyde's impotence in the earlier film developing into Luc's bi-/homosexuality in need of 'unblocking', the legendary American pair's

father–son union are revelled in with a semi-pornographic candour not seen anywhere else in Ozon's œuvre: young Luc's deflowering by the gruff, bearded ogre takes a taboo dynamic merely flirted with in *La Petite Mort* and *Le Temps qui reste* and transforms it into the widely disseminated dream-work of a French gay Oedipus.[17] The soundtrack of *Les Amants criminels* is the first of Ozon's truly ambitious attempts to create a musical counterpoint to a set of images that dazzles in its intensity and heterogeneity. From the softly knowing trip-hop of Lamb (as Luc and Alice, like so many other Ozonian protagonists, calmly roam supermarket aisles in search of their desires – here, a shovel) to the overwrought strings of Philippe Rombi's original score, which builds to a near-deafening climax during the final chase sequence, the tunes that serve as the backdrop to the characters' adventures rise and swell in a manner that announces Ozon's cinema as anything but subtle and retiring. As for the figure of Alice, played by Natacha Regnier (fresh from her 1998 Cannes-winning triumph in Erick Zonca's *La Vie rêvée des anges*), she starts detractors once and for all on the question of Ozon's potential misogyny. Why *does* he seem to take such delight in portraits of female cruelty, perversion and destruction? This charge seems to dog Ozon almost as much as its equally stark opposite: the gushing assertion (upheld by none more vehemently than Ozon himself) that, on the contrary, here is a film director who simply loves women. The films themselves contain a far more complex sexual politics than either position actually allows.[18]

---

compulsive criminality becoming the modern French couple's schoolyard fantasies.

17 Ozon enthusiastically notes the film's sexual function: 'En tout cas, je sais que le film est assez excitant pour les homos. J'ai un copain qui m'a dit qu'il voulait acheter le même lit que l'ogre, avec les barreaux en fer' ('Either way, I know the film is quite a turn-on for gay men. A friend of mine told me he wanted to buy the same bed as the ogre, with the iron bars', Doustaly, 1999).

18 Ozon insists in nearly every interview he gives upon his profound 'identification' with all his women – Alice, Marie, Marion, Angel and the rest, going so far as to state, a propos of his link to the protagonist of *Swimming Pool*, 'Oui, c'est un autoportrait' (Marvier, 2003: 15). This position (understandably) does not appear to satisfy the harsher critics: 'Que les actrices se précipitent dans ce piège en en redemandant en dit long sur leur masochisme ... On a presque du mal à appeler ça de la misogynie tant la méchanceté d'Ozon à l'égard de la femme est compliquée' ('That actresses should rush into this trap and ask for more says a lot about their masochism ... Ozon's nastiness with regard to women is so complicated it almost makes it difficult to call it misogyny', Azoury, 2007).

'Un petit divertissement à quatre': *Gouttes d'eau sur pierres brûlantes* (1999)

Having established, by the age of 32, such a seemingly incontrovertible identity as a highly personal *auteur* working exclusively from his own scripts or original ideas, it may have seemed surprising when Ozon announced in 1999 that he was adapting Rainer Werner Fassbinder's play *Tropfen auf heisse Steine* (*Water Drops on Burning Rocks*), written in the mid-1960s when Fassbinder was just 19, and regarded by him as a piece of juvenilia, never to be put on stage. According to Ozon, the play was exactly what he was looking for at that moment: 'Depuis longtemps je voulais faire un film sur un couple, sur la difficulté de vivre à deux et de supporter le quotidien. En découvrant la pièce de Fassbinder au théâtre j'ai réalisé que je n'avais pas besoin d'écrire un scénario, puisque cette pièce existait, et qu'elle correspondait à ce que j'avais envie de raconter' ('For a long time I had wanted to make a film about a couple, about the difficulty of living as two and dealing with the everyday. When I discovered this Fassbinder play at the theatre, I realised I didn't need to write a script since this play existed and it corresponded to what I wanted to relate', Grant, 2000). This was the first time Ozon adapted a pre-existing text, but it proved to be a practice he pulled off rather well, later demonstrating with *8 femmes* and (somewhat less successfully) *Angel* his apparent delight in finding obscure and forgotten pieces and breathing Ozonian life into them. Of all directors, it is Rainer Werner Fassbinder whom Ozon repeatedly claims to have had the most influence on his cinematic vision.[19] The extreme cruelty of Fassbinder's vision of human relations, the artifice with which he presents his universe, the heightened emotional register within which his stories unfold and the sexual mobility of his characters are all hallmarks that we immediately recognise in Ozon's own work. Rather than construct a slavish filmic homage to the German's play, however, with *Gouttes d'eau* Ozon boldly remodels the original narrative and emphasis in order to construct quite a different piece, as much an Ozon 'original' as anything else in his filmography, yet weirdly impregnated with a myriad of elements lifted from *other*

---

19 In addition to his numerous citations, a mark of Ozon's devotion to the German director is that in 2005 he took part (alongside regular performers in Fassbinder's films such as Hanna Schygulla and Ingrid Craven) in an international conference devoted to Fassbinder's work held at the Centre Pompidou in Paris.

Fassbinder films. The result is an utterly singular piece of contemporary French filmmaking: filmed in French, yet set in Germany of the 1970s, it boasts a stylistic discordance reminiscent of Fassbinder's own bizarre German western (set in nineteenth-century America) *Whity* (1970). Once again using a non-French actress in a key role (Anna Thomson, fresh from her triumphs in Amos Kollek's classic art-house portraits of contemporary feminine despair in New York, *Sue* and *Fiona*, both 1998) Ozon continues to indulge his predilection for the exploration of national and gender (Thomson plays a transsexual) identities poised very much on a knife edge. Perhaps most importantly, in turning to Fassbinder for inspiration, Ozon allows himself to transpose his fascination with the multiple layers and implications of sadomasochistic living from his recent immersion in a world of demon hikers and forest ogres to the 'normal' environment of men and women (and those in between) in love. The result is no less violently upsetting.

Franz (Malik Zidi), a handsome, sensitive, serious student, 19 years old and in a stable relationship with his girlfriend, is picked up one evening by Leopold Blum (Bernard Giraudeau), a suave, 50-year-old businessman. Quickly falling for Leopold's seductive charm, Franz finds himself, as if by magic, living with the older man, keeping house for him, desperately, hopelessly in love. Leopold, meanwhile, has turned nasty. Snapping constantly at his young worshipper, he returns Franz's love only with wrath, contempt and occasional violence. The two continue to have a mutually fulfilling sex life, however. Franz's loneliness and depression become increasingly acute, romantic music and poetry seemingly the only outlets for his strangled, seeping, bleeding emotions. He threatens repeatedly to leave, but never quite makes it out of the house. Leopold is unsympathetic, accusing Franz of distracting him from his work (to which he is devoted), and suggesting callously that Franz prostitute himself to bring in some extra cash. While Leopold is away on an extended business trip, Franz is paid an unexpected visit by his former girlfriend, the childlike Anna (Ludivine Sagnier). Professing still to be in love with him, and begging him to come away with her before she marries someone else, she convinces him to leave Leopold, and the two have sex, despite Franz's coldness, emotional withdrawal, disturbing (if unconvincing) imitations of Leopold's verbal cruelty and frank, tear-soaked admission that he will never be able to love anyone but Leopold, who at that point arrives home unexpectedly. Commanding Franz to make him some coffee, Leopold sets about seducing the easily impressed Anna, who succumbs without the slightest resistance. Just then, the doorbell rings: it is Vera (Anna Thomson), a mysterious woman in dark glasses and furs, who has already appeared twice before at the door asking for Leopold, only to find first Franz, then Anna. Now Vera is admitted entry: Leopold reveals that she is an ex-lover of his, a former man, who has undergone a sex-change operation in Casablanca. At this point Leopold's authority swells beyond recognition. After choreographing a short dance routine in which all four participate, and in the course of which he shines, he orders Anna and Vera to the bedroom, and invites a broken Franz to join them. Franz declines, and fantasises about killing Leopold with a revolver. Vera (who has been ignored in bed by Leopold and Anna) finds Franz lying in the other room, wrapped in her fur coat. The two talk for a while about the nature of love and suffering, and Vera tells Franz her story: once a boy, desperately in love with Leopold, she changed her sex in order to appease Leopold's constant need for novelty, before finding herself thrown out into the street by Leopold some time afterwards. Vera suggests tentatively that she and Franz attempt to form a couple together, but it is too late: Franz has poisoned himself and is about to die. He telephones his mother, who wishes him a 'bon voyage'. When he is dead, Vera alerts Leopold and Anna. Anna shrieks in horror, but is commanded by Leopold to go back to the bedroom, which she does. Leopold manifests only irritation at the situation, and goes back into the bedroom with Anna. He invites Vera to join them, but she remains with Franz's corpse. She tries to open the window, but finds she cannot.

Ozon not only retains the theatrical element of the original play, but heightens this sense of artifice wherever he can. The film is divided into four 'acts', each announced by intertitle on a black screen. The characters' movements are highly stylised, choreographed so atten-tively that at times they appear to be dancing rather than moving naturally. The preposterous dance sequence three-quarters of the way through the film (which we will discuss at greater length in Chapter 4) takes the film's anti-naturalism to its climax. Ozon's predilection for the cinematic creation of a sense of life performed rather than lived can be helpfully understood as arising not so much from a need to establish himself as the 1990s progeny of Godard (à la Tarantino) as from a desire to create a world in which characters have immersed themselves so deeply in fantasy and ritual that, rather as in a Genet play, their very surroundings have taken on the air of overt and unashamed spectacle. Franz, Leopold, Anna and Vera are (or so they think) expert performers within narratives of their own making. And, indeed, Franz will exclaim, in his first moments of real lucidity near the film's climax: 'Vous êtes comme des marionettes!' ('You're like puppets!'). The problem with dwelling within fantasy – and here, as we may expect, the fantasy is an explicitly sadomasochistic one – is that, while the players may believe that they can manipulate and alter their roles within it to suit their needs at a given time, the non-negotiable horror at the heart of the apparently show-like situation is altogether less flexible. Thus Franz may take comfort from the superficial elasticity of aspects of his sadomasochistic play with Leopold: the two men swap the lines of the initial night together, reversing the roles they inhabited that first time, and re-enacting the fundamental fantasy at the heart of their relation – seduction by one's stepfather – with delight. Later, even Anna will occupy the role of the little boy/girl who lies naked on the bed, waiting for her daddy to arrive in a long overcoat. And yet what soon becomes patently clear is that no matter how many times the lines and roles get turned around, ultimately only Leopold really gets to be the 'daddy', only Leopold wields the authority sufficient to control all the situations within the household, both in the bedroom and outside it. The line-swapping game is of no lasting consequence whatsoever. By the same token, Franz may enjoy a certain flexibility of role inherent in his apparently unproblematic bisexuality: he shifts from Anna's boyfriend to Leopold's boy and back again. This flexibility might suggest a willing, chosen element in his new status in Act Two as Leopold's domestic slave, dressed in the ridiculous garb of a 7-year-old Bavarian schoolboy. But as the film goes on we realise that we simply cannot speak of anything like choice in the position Franz has come to occupy. Like one of the accursed party guests who inexplicably cannot leave the party in Buñuel's *The Exterminating Angel* (1962), Franz really does seem trapped: he will only leave Leopold's house when he is dead. Ozon talks of the ways in which aspects of the actors' dress and appearance communicate a constant shifting and transferability: each actor's hairstyle changes, for example, as the film progresses, sometimes quite improbably so. Clothes are handed on from one character to another in a sort of chain of transmission: Anna wears Leopold's dressing gown, while

Franz dies in Vera's fur coat. Again, though, this is a purely superficial mobility: closer analysis of what is ultimately the film's logic reveals an essential fixity of roles, with Leopold retaining (and expanding) his initial position of dominance throughout, and with the other three occupying varying degrees of subservience. When Franz attempts to speak to Anna as though he possessed the masterfulness of Leopold, the effect is tragic, pathetic. Malik Zidi's astonishingly generous, open performance – broad smiles, cascading tears, eyes searching to connect – and thin, fragile physique communicates instead a character in whom an intractable vulnerability resides, and which no amount of self-conscious role-playing can overcome.[20] By contrast, Bernard Giraudeau as Leopold conveys an effortless dominance from start to finish. Far bulkier, and obviously older, than Zidi, he overwhelms him with his very physical presence. The two actors use a very different body language, Zidi all uncontainable, overflowing, nervous energy, Giraudeau all calm, self-possessed smoothness, punctuated by the occasional outburst of violent fury.[21] When, in the seduction scene of Act One, Ozon's smoothly circular tracking camera films Leopold/Giraudeau smoothly circling and tracking Franz/Zidi in the opposite direction, we once again get the impression that the holder of power in this film is no longer human, but rather a beast of prey, hunting down its weakly nervous victim with all the confidence of a panther. When, in the opening scene of Act Three, Ozon's motionless camera films Leopold sodomising an ecstatically grateful Franz from behind, the viewer is left with the impression that s/he has witnessed a mortal being enraptured by a god. Leopold's unexpected arrival just as Anna

20 It is useful, by way of illustration of this 'open' style of acting, to contrast the way in which Zidi plays Franz smoking alone in the bath with other bath smokers in Ozon's films (it is a recurring leitmotif). Unlike Marina de Van (in *Regarde la mer*), Ludivine Sagnier (in *Swimming Pool*) and Melvil Poupaud (in *Le Temps qui reste*), all of whom retain a deliberately inscrutable expression even as they savour the sensuality of their solitary pleasure, Zidi smiles as he stares off into his fantasy-soaked middle distance, reciting lines of poetry in German to himself or to an imaginary lover. Zidi, as Franz, never stops trying to connect, even when alone. After many nominations for Best Male Newcomer at the French César awards (in 2000 for Ozon's *Gouttes d'eau*, in 2003 for Antoine Santana's *Un Moment de bonheur* and in 2005 for André Téchiné's *Les Temps qui changent*), the apparently permanent newcomer Zidi won this award in 2007 for Emmanuel Bourdieu's *Les Amitiés maléfiques*.

21 The actors' real-life *rapport de forces*, Zidi the shy newcomer, Giraudeau the established star, mirrors and intensifies this contrast.

believes she is getting Franz to leave with her brilliantly echoes the ogre's arrival at the hut and capture of Luc and Alice before they can escape in *Les Amants criminels*. This film may be set in 1970s West Germany, but its characters are no less phantasmagoric than those of the French fairy tale.[22]

If there is one truly inescapable process of subjugation into which Franz, Anna and Vera appear to be increasingly cemented and which the film, far more ambitiously even than Fassbinder's original play, seems determined to explore, it is that of their shared feminisation. One of the reasons Leopold's power within the household retains such vigour is because he is the only one of the four characters to enjoy an unproblematically 'masculine' subject position. The other three each perch on different branches of an artificial – but horribly tenacious – 'femininity'. Franz, from the start of Act Two, has begun to be pushed into the activities, attitudes and neuroses traditionally associated with women living in patriarchal societies. He spends his days cleaning the house, anxiously attempting – terrified that Leopold will leave him for a better model – to maintain his youthful good looks, and engaging Leopold in fruitless dialogues in which clearly all he desires is to be reassured that he is loved. Often wandering around in his underwear – like Anna and Vera – he is the camera's object, Zidi's body offered up as much for the viewer's protracted judgement as Franz's is for Leopold's. When Ludivine Sagnier makes her entrance as Anna half-way through the film, the viewer is intrigued to see what the power positioning of this 'real' female will be in an all-male context where the men simply inhabit greater or lesser degrees of masculine power. At first it seems that, in the misogynistic order of things, her exaggerated 'girliness' (Sagnier's high-pitched, cartoonish voice and blonde schoolgirl mop are highly comical when she first appears) will place her even lower down in the household hierarchy than Franz.[23] And yet, ultimately, even if Anna does end up as merely the latest of Leopold's young toys, she appears to sustain

22 It is useful to note that the deliberately socio-political detail offered by Fassbinder (with regard to Leopold's character in particular: his apparent Jewishness, his quasi-obsessive devotion to capitalism) is downplayed by Ozon, always more comfortable with a dehistoricised and depoliticised fantasy space it would seem.

23 It is amusing to note in passing that, at least according to Ozon's commentary on the DVD, Sagnier did voices for cartoon rabbits on French children's television.

far less violence than Franz. It is as though her full and non-ironic immersion in her condition of abased 'female' serves somehow to protect her from lasting pain. Franz's torture seems to proceed from an awareness of – and thus a certain distance from – the servile position he inhabits. He has fallen into the horror of Leopold's real sadism, wrecked against the rocks of a faulty belief in the possibility of negotiating humiliation and its (here) concomitant condition: feminisation. His continuing Romantic anguish – a sensibility by which Anna seems entirely unaffected, comically illustrated as she merrily hums a song (Françoise Hardy's 'Träume', which we will discuss in more detail in Chapter Four) that is clearly tearing Franz's very soul apart – stems from this mistaken belief that things could, somehow, have gone a different way. The 'femininity' of the transsexual Vera appears to have far more in common with that of Franz.[24] She too has apparently chosen the servile condition she now lives: according to the values of most postmodern cultural theory, Vera exemplifies the freedom and disconcerting hybridity of the border-crossing, 'decentred' subject. And yet, as usual in Ozon's cinema, there can ultimately be no glibness for the transgressing individual, no freedom in the adoption of voluntary servitude. For Vera's apparent flexibility, like that of Franz, is rendered rigid and unworkable, the path simply to a limitless exposure to pain, failing as it does to smooth over the ultimate non-negotiable vulnerability: love and the need to be loved.[25] The similarity in Franz's and Vera's particular relation to pain is something Ozon's alterations to Fassbinder's play seem determined to underline, through the long dialogue he allows the two to enjoy (in which the viewer understands that Vera is Franz's potential future self), the coat Vera leaves Franz's corpse wrapped in ('comme si elle y laissait sa propre peau', as Ozon puts it – 'as if she were leaving

24 In Fassbinder's original play Vera was a 'real' woman. Ozon is perhaps inspired to turn her into a transsexual by Fassbinder's remarkable 1978 film *In a Year of Thirteen Moons*.

25 Vera is one of many recent cinematic transsexuals whom theorists often, perhaps admirably, try to turn into heroines of postmodern reversibility, but who may, upon closer analysis, embody a horrifyingly static lack of agency. The character of Frédéric/Viviane (played by French heart-throb Vincent Perez) in Patrice Chéreau's *Ceux qui m'aiment prendront le train* (1998) and, rather more compellingly, Pedro Almodóvar's venerable trinity of Tina (*Law of Desire*, 1987), Agrado (*All about my Mother*, 1999) and Ignacio (*Bad Education*, 2004) all deserve ample critical consideration.

her own skin there'), and Vera's almost bewitched inability to open the window in the film's final frame (Ozon's cruellest films always seem to take place in Sadeian *huis clos*). The two pain-riddled *femmes manquées* are sealed together more tightly still by Zidi and Thomson's acting styles – she playing as painfully 'openly' as he – which sublimely mirror and complement the other's gaping wounds.

Gynocritical cinema: *8 femmes* (2001)

Ozon's films usually sow within their overall portrait of power relations important sub-questions which have significant repercussions for specifically feminist readings of his work. How is it possible to negotiate a feminine or significantly feminised identity within a social framework at the unreachable centre of which sits a silent, bland or indifferent patriarch? And is it preferable that this 'silent father' be made to transform, somehow, into a monstrous ogre of depravity before one can truly encounter or confront him? This cocktail of neo-Lacanian interrogations reached its improbable landmark climax when in 2001 he adapted Robert Thomas's quaintly banal stage play *8 femmes* for the screen. Ozon had originally wanted to film a remake of George Cukor's 1939 MGM classic *The Women*, but discovered that Meg Ryan and Julia Roberts owned the rights. Abandoning this project, he discovered the existence of Thomas's 1960s detective drama, thanks to the actor and agent Dominique Besnehard: Ozon decided that this would do just as well for what he had in mind (Ozon, 2002: 21). Released in France in 2002 and nominated for a clutch of César awards, *8 femmes* is, to date, far and away Ozon's most commercially successful film, and the project that serves as the most obvious watershed in his career at the time of writing. The huge impact it had on the French (and international) cinematic landscape can be attributed, it is fairly safe to suggest, less to its unusually polished exploration of political and psychoanalytical quandaries (Hain, 2007: 278) describes the film as 'a scathing Marxist analysis of the anti-human nature of capitalism, and the collusion of capitalism and patriarchy to keep women dependent') than to its highly original (and deeply entertaining) exploitation of the musical genre (an issue to which we shall return in Chapter Four) and its incredible (and predictably much-discussed) acquisition for its all-female cast of some of the most important icons and artists of the French cinema. That Ozon was able to assemble a cast that included Fanny Ardant, Emmanuelle Béart, Danielle Darrieux, Catherine Deneuve and Isabelle Huppert was generally taken as a bona fide sign that he had finally 'arrived' as a director, only 34 years old, yet able to command the collective respect of actresses who had cut their teeth with the undisputed masters (and a mistress) of a French golden age: Buñuel, Carné, Chabrol, Demy, Godard, Pialat, Resnais, Rivette, Téchiné, Truffaut and Varda. The basic Agatha Christie-style murder plot is, for the most part, pure hokum. But, as with his previous and subsequent adaptations, *Gouttes d'eau sur pierres brûlantes* and *Angel*, Ozon (this time assisted on the screenplay by Marina de Van) feels free to alter all manner of details, making of that basic plot the most purely irrelevant 'MacGuffin' for a long time in film history. He inserts eight songs, absent from the original play, plucked from several decades of French pop history, and incongruously performed, to the spectator's stupefaction, by each of the eight actresses; he spreads out a dazzling array of intertextual cinematic allusions; he implants deeply inappropriate references to sexual, sadomasochistic and broadly transgressive desires, desires that impregnate each and every character and relation. In short, Ozon transforms Thomas's drably innocuous play into a bright pink candy box of pulsating kitsch, perversion and sweet-smelling cruelty.

The film, like the play, takes place on one day in a large, French, bourgeois country house some time in the 1950s. Suzon (Virginie Ledoyen), the 19-year-old eldest daughter, comes home for Christmas, freshly returned from studies in England. She is warmly welcomed by her glamorous mother Gaby (Catherine Deneuve), the devoted housekeeper Mme Chanel (Firmine Richard), her wheelchair-bound grandmother Mamy (Danielle Darrieux) and her excitable younger sister Catherine (Ludivine Sagnier), receives a frostily critical reception from her unmarried aunt Augustine (Isabelle Huppert) and an impenetrable one from the coolly beautiful new maid Louise (Emmanuelle Béart). Gaby's husband, the master of the house Marcel, is apparently asleep in his bedroom, worn out from business activities. Catherine performs a light-hearted ditty ('Papa, t'es plus dans le coup') about the obsolescence of paternal authority, but the cheery atmosphere is soon interrupted by a scream from Louise, who announces that the master Marcel is dead in his bed, a dagger in his back. It is also discovered that the telephone line has been cut.

Everyone is shocked, but Suzon soon takes charge, asking everyone to cooperate and answer her questions, since it is possible that one of them is the murderer. Barely suppressed tensions soon arise, and Augustine, sick of being treated with contempt by her richer, more glamorous sister Gaby, bites, claws, and breaks a vase in fury, before singing a confessional ballad ('Message personnel') about the undying love for everyone she feels deep inside. A stranger appears in the garden, and makes her way to the house: it is Pierrette (Fanny Ardant), Marcel's sister, long-banished by Gaby owing to her apparent immorality and her disreputable profession of exotic dancer. Pierrette claims she has received a call from an anonymous woman informing her of her brother's death, before marching into Marcel's room to see the body for herself, then performing a cabaret-style piece about the single woman's life ('A quoi sert de vivre libre?') to the bemused other seven women. The women, still being interrogated by Suzon, come up with various alibis for their whereabouts the previous night, though Suzon herself is tripped up, and must confess that she in fact went to see her father in the early hours, to tell him of her pregnancy. Gaby is appalled, but Suzon sings a charmingly bittersweet tune to Catherine about her baby's mysterious father ('Toi, mon amour, mon ami') in their bedroom. The women continue to bicker and fight among themselves. Augustine has a hysterical fit and demands to be injected in the behind by anyone: Louise administers the needle. It is revealed by Louise that Mme Chanel and Pierrette are old friends and card partners, and Mme Chanel confesses her romantic love for Pierrette, before being banished to the kitchen in a cloud of repulsion, where she sings a sad ballad about the loneliness of life ('Pour ne pas vivre seul'). Gaby confesses to Suzon (at Pierrette's instigation) that she herself gave birth to Suzon out of wedlock and that Marcel was not her real father. Later Mme Chanel insists she knows the whole truth about Marcel's murder but, before she can reveal it, she is silenced by a gunshot that does not wound her but nevertheless sends her into catatonia. It is revealed that Louise and Marcel had been having an affair, and Louise sings Augustine a mocking number ('Pile ou face'), designed to demonstrate what it means to have true feminine sex appeal. A drunken Mamy (long-since risen from her wheelchair) confesses to Augustine that she killed her daughters' father many years ago, whereupon both Augustine and Mamy go berserk, and Gaby is forced to knock out her mother with a bottle, before shoving her in the cupboard, and attempting sisterly reconciliation with the distraught Augustine. Augustine undergoes an image transformation, dressing in the glamorous attire of Gaby and removing her glasses. Meanwhile, Louise stops performing certain of her domestic duties, lets her hair down, leers increasingly openly at her mistress Gaby, and suggests not only that she was the maid and lover of her former mistress (she shows a photograph of the dead actress Romy Schneider), but also that she does not do her present menial job out of economic necessity but out of desire. Suzon reveals to Catherine that her baby has been fathered by Marcel, whom she had believed at the time to be her own father. Things build towards their climax: Pierrette and Gaby have a final private showdown, in the course of which Gaby sings a torch song of despairing love ('Toi, jamais'), and in which it is revealed that both women have been having an affair with the same man, Marcel's business partner Jacques Arnoux, and that Pierrette was also her brother Marcel's lover. The sisters-in-law fight on the carpet but end up in sexual embrace. Finally Mme Chanel speaks again and demands that Catherine reveal the truth: the young girl and her father had staged the whole murder as a test for the seven women and are now going to move away together. As Catherine runs to Marcel's bedroom to fetch him, he shoots himself in the head. Mamy sings a final lament for life and love ('Il n'y a pas d'amour heureux') to her youngest granddaughter and the other women, before all eight women dance in pairs and line up in unity.

When discussing his early feelings about the project that would become his film of *8 femmes*, Ozon mentions his childhood love of dolls and of doll's houses (Ozon, 2002: 20). The remark is potentially far more interesting than an amusingly camp gesture. It captures what is at stake in so many of Ozon's films and happens merely to be exemplified in *8 femmes*: Ozon's characters, along with the actors that play them, are so often puppet-like creatures in his doll-loving hands, sadistically prodded and pulled – rather like the dead parents of *Victor* – to perform whatever function the grown-up boy director wants to see enacted. With *8 femmes*, the entire landscape of the film might be helpfully considered as a sadomasochistic game with life-size doll victims. For the most part the actresses are directed – complying with a remarkably self-renouncing amenability – to deliver performances that not only reflect ironically but also parody and debase their already existing star images. Catherine Deneuve's (largely misperceived) cultural image of studied elegance, conservatism and hypocritical sexual repression is toyed with here to make Deneuve/Gaby (the two are utterly conflated) into a truly grotesque frump, 'toujours belle après toutes ces années' perhaps, but in a manner so artificial that she borders on monstrosity. The 'real' Deneuve of interviews and photo shoots is, ironically, far more youthful and 'human' looking.[26] Isabelle Huppert's increasingly neurotic star image of the 1990s is pushed to its limit, turning her here into a comical bundle of hysterical symptoms, twitching and flailing convulsively at every movement of the camera.[27] When Augustine/Huppert finally descends the staircase with make-up, loose hair and Gaby's fur coat, the effect is more risible than beautifying. Danielle Darrieux's controversial wartime activities (she notoriously participated in a theatrical tour of Nazi Germany) sit only too well with her on-screen incarnation as an old, selfish, reactionary murderess, whose smashing on the head with a bottle functions as important vengeful catharsis for the Deneuve–Huppert generation.[28]

If the actresses themselves can be viewed as dolls in a somewhat sadomasochistic (yet presumably pleasurable) game between them and Ozon, their intra-diegetic characters are no less caught up in the machinations of violently desiring games and role-play. All the charac-

26 A further 'game' Ozon plays with Deneuve's star image is in his cinematic transformation of Gaby not only into an object of (Louise's) lesbian desire but also into a closet lesbian herself. Deneuve is well known as a slightly problematic 'lesbian icon', enthusiastically playing lesbian roles (as in André Téchiné's 1996 film *Les Voleurs* and Tony Scott's 1983 film *The Hunger*) but alienating many lesbians with her successful suing of the unfortunately named lesbian publication *Deneuve* (see Asibong: 2007).

27 Huppert's eponymous role in Michael Haneke's controversial 2001 film version of Elfriede Jelinek's *The Piano Teacher* is a particularly obvious reference point: like Huppert's award-winning dramatic persona in that film, Erika Kohut, Huppert's Augustine is a piano-playing, masturbatory, sharp-tongued spinster who exists in a peculiarly intimate relationship with her widowed mother.

28 The piece in the *Cahiers du cinéma* on *8 femmes* claims, compellingly, that 'le véritable objet du film est chirurgical; il s'agit d'opérer des greffes, des hybridations et des déplacements à partir de la mémoire cinématographique véhiculée par chaque actrice' ('the film's veritable function is surgical; it sets out to perform transplants, cross-fertilisations and realignments, using the cinematic memory conveyed by each actress as its starting point'), before going on to assert that 'Ozon a réalisé le film le plus délibérément *méta* du cinéma français' ('Ozon has made the most deliberately *meta* film in French cinema history', Lalanne, 2002: 82–3).

ters can be seen to act out their desire through ritual, to a far more exaggerated, self-aware, and perverse degree than Robert Thomas ever dreamed of in his original play. The theatrical hugs and kisses Mamy, Gaby, Catherine and Suzon share in the film's early scenes will soon give way to equally jerky and anti-naturalistic fights; Mamy's paralysis of the legs is soon revealed as a kind of performance, when (like *Sitcom*'s Sophie) she leaps from the wheel-chair to run up the stairs after Augustine; Suzon's words of virginal, rose-tinted, conventional morality morph unexpectedly into deadpan declarations of sexual love for her 'father' lover. Ozon stages almost every sequence of the film with the utmost artificiality. When Augustine develops her hysterical crisis, screaming, braying for her injection ('ma piqûre!'), the whole procedure is filmed as a kind of collective – simultaneously comic and obscene – dance, one more 'number' in the film, simply minus a song this time. Ozon's camera tracks Béart, Richard, Sagnier and Darrieux carrying Huppert into the kitchen, before cutting to a highly stagey argument between Deneuve and Ledoyen which is then applauded by Ardant, cutting back to the spectacle of the injection: a medium shot of the two maids, the grandmother and granddaughter holding down the flailing 'hysteric', whose knickers, buttocks, stockings and suspenders dominate the lower half of the frame, and whose sexual groans ('Ah, c'est bon!') as the needle penetrates her flesh are heard over a close-up shot of Huppert's orgasmically trembling head. The characters in this film are, then, perhaps more excessively than in any other Ozon film, steeped in sadomasochistic performances for each other's benefit, performances which they appear, to a large extent, themselves to be manipulating. Huppert's character in the injection sequence seems to have staged the entire situation as a masochistic death fantasy that will encourage the pity of all those around her at the same time as giving her immense erotic pleasure. The character who seems at first glance most removed from Huppert's Augustine, the lascivious maid Louise, played by Béart, is similarly fascinated by the possibilities both of exciting sympathy through melodramatic statements of vulnerability (she moans of her near-death to mistress Gaby upon her return from the snow) and of elaborating explicitly sexualised sadomasochistic situations. Positively quivering with excitement as Gaby barks at her to go and look for her injection kit, she will later turn on her 'maîtresse' for not displaying *enough* authority. Louise uses an explicitly sadomasochistic discourse, with built-in assumptions of reversibility and improvisation, to perplex and destabilise the paradigms of power distribution upon which the *bourgeoise* Gaby – utterly taken aback – depends to maintain her superiority. Augustine and Louise, on the surface so different, both use SM performance and play to express their own desire and to confound those around them. That they should share the film's most playfully sadomasochistic scenes together (the injection and the 'Pile ou face' sequence where Louise ritualistically and musically humiliates a fascinated Augustine) is entirely fitting.

And yet – as always with Ozon's films involving 'playful' pain – a closer analysis of the way in which Ozon and de Van's screenplay adaptation functions reveals a greater, far more inflexible machine of power at work. This machine is effortlessly manned, of course, by the dead-alive figure of Marcel. The shocking alterations made to Robert Thomas's original play are, as we should by now be starting to understand is the case with almost all of Ozon's shock tactics, far from facile or gratuitous. By inserting a variety of ever-more allegedly transgressive postures, attitudes and dispositions embodied and performed by the eight women – rebelliousness in Catherine, promiscuity in Pierrette, adultery in Gaby, lesbianism in Mme Chanel, Louise, Gaby and Pierrette, hysteria in Augustine, murderousness in Mamy, incest in Suzon and Pierrette, sadomasochistic drives in Louise and Augustine – the viewer is led at first towards an appreciation of the film as vastly more liberating for its female characters than the 1960s original play (or than its 1930s cinematic older sister, *The Women*), a perversely postmodern saunter through an incongruous 1950s landscape in which the women, bizarrely, are able to access all the 'lifestyle options' that we would expect from the most libertarian of societies. Yet it is precisely in this updating, in this offering to his women of an apparently chosen perversity, that Ozon demonstrates more unshakably still the apparent solidity of the invisible father's position as the ultimate wielder of authority and generator of desire. As the film progresses, we come to realise not only Marcel's absolute indifference when alive to postures that might feasibly be conceived as assaults on his power – indeed he is often revealed as the monstrous instigator of many of these – but also the lack of freedom his 'death' has brought about. The women are, more than ever, in thrall to his memory, to his fantasy, to the empty signifier 'Papa'. This continued prostration to the name of the father despite everything results only in the women's turning on each other in a generalised, decidedly non-playful cult of sadism. Louise and Augustine's instances of sadomasochistic pleasure are as nothing compared to the constant proliferation of serious wounds nearly all the characters suffer and visit upon one another. More striking even than the multitude of slaps, punches and blows to the head Ozon films with an emotionally detached coolness from start to (nearly) finish, are the various, socially mediated, linguistic humiliations in which the characters indulge, with a decidedly non-ironic view to inflicting grave injury. These insults are usually based on misogynistic, homophobic, often simply fascistic values, spouted by the 'transgressive' women with the utmost ease. Thus Mme Chanel is upbraided in horror as 'une invertie' (even though at least half of the remaining characters also have decidedly lesbian tendencies); Louise is dismissed by the herself lowly Pierrette with the insult 'Vous n'êtes qu'une bonne' ('You're only a maid'); Catherine finds that the gravest fault of which she can accuse her sister is frigidity, and her aunt virginity. Each of the women seems stuck for much of the film within a particular discourse that lies at the root of a particular strain of politically inflected cruelty. Louise is fond of theories and clichés that border on fascism in their insistence on the value of social function and the truth of eternal femininity and incontrovertible authority. Gaby seems to be the voice of 'moderate' conservatism, constantly telling those she considers socially weak to be grateful for her hospitality. Most fascinatingly, Suzon embodies the oppressiveness of 'liberal' values, busily mouthing platitudes about tolerance and the importance of family unity while at the same time manipulating those around her into confessing their sins as she herself carefully covers up her own position of enunciation, conveniently 'forgetting' to interrogate herself. During her quizzing of the other seven women, Ozon's camera remains for much of the time on Suzon's back, emphasising the way in which she cleverly conceals her own true face from the assembly through her adoption of the guise of kindly law maker. The weirdly disturbing, even *Salò*-like inability of the collectively victimised group to find any solidarity within the experience of their group humiliation is implicit (if perhaps not especially seriously thought through) in Thomas's original play: we laugh when Pierrette humiliates Augustine over her secret penchant for romantic novels, when Mme Chanel bad-mouths her servant colleague Louise or when Louise betrays Pierrette's and Chanel's secret rendezvous. But Ozon's camera delights in accentuating this phenomenon in visual terms. The debasement of one woman is watched by the other seven – and by the camera – with the utmost delectation. Firmine Richard as the endlessly humiliated Mme Chanel elicits some of the most striking examples of this objectification. 'Outed' as a lesbian before the horrified gaze of Gaby, Mamy and Suzon – and the unsympathetic one of her lover Pierrette – Chanel is pushed onto her knees (by Pierrette): a medium shot of her tear-stained face facing towards the camera, partially blocked by the arm of a looming Deneuve as Gaby, standing over her, her back to the camera, functions as a perfect metonym for the visual isolation and singularisation of a given character in this film. A shot later, Ozon's *mise-en-scène* captures, in very slightly low-angled long shot, Richard/Chanel, still on her knees, her back to the camera, surrounded on all sides by the standing Ardant/Pierrette, Deneuve/Gaby, Ledoyen/Suzon and (in a wheelchair, but still imperiously raised above Chanel) Mamy/Darrieux. The faces of the erect women are all visible. Later, just before and during Chanel's gun accident, her isolation from the entire (for once, superficially bonded) group becomes more striking still: as she scurries outside the house and then back in again, the would-be triumphant bearer of the truth, the others decide to hide and observe her. Capturing her alone, in perplexed medium shot at the house's threshold, Ozon's camera participates – with the other hiding characters as well as with the spectator – in the sadistic scrutiny of her lone figure. Once the shot has been fired and the hidden voyeurs leap out of their hiding places, a famous, motionless, 15-second high-angle shot from Chanel's perspective frames the other seven women bending over her in horrified fascination, briefly united in their collective act of bullying.[29]

By the time of the film's final frame (the incredible line-up of the eight women holding hands, on the verge of a bow, the transmitters of the first sensation of something like peace and cohesion since the film's start) Marcel's despotic figure – equally monstrous when alive or believed dead – seems, somehow, to have been sufficiently bled of its sadistic power to allow for the possibility of new relations beyond

29 This isolation of Mme Chanel from the other seven women is unfortunately echoed in the isolation of the actress Firmine Richard from the other seven performers: rarely mentioned in reviews of the film and without fail placed last in the cast list, much of the marketing of *8 femmes* proceeded as though the eighth woman simply did not exist.

his spectre. How are viewers to interpret this image of an improbably sudden togetherness, not unlike the final shots of *Sitcom*, in which Hélène, Maria, Abdu, Nicolas, Sophie and David come together for the first time in a spirit of love and tranquillity at the Jean-Rat's funeral? Can films such as *Sitcom* and *8 femmes* – or even *Une Rose entre nous* and *Une Robe d'été* – take seriously the notion that such paradigms of new community are attainable following the necessary passages through mobility, pain and various combinations of music, emotion and horror? Or does Ozon mock us for even pondering such an optimistic reading of his films' (often strikingly analogous) climactic plunges from solitude with fantasy to relation with something else? As Mark Hain (2007: 288) puts it with admirable clarity, 'the very ambiguity (what [Robin] Wood refers to as the resolution the films can never achieve on their own) in the films of both Hitchcock and Ozon speaks to the necessity of engaged and questioning viewership. What each filmmaker presents to us can be received as a didactic, pre-packaged message, or as a vital and challenging critique: the difference is in the viewer'. The ultimate power, it would seem, then, lies with us.

References

Asibong, Andrew (2007) 'The killing of sister Catherine: Deneuve's lesbian transformations', *From Perversion to Purity: The Stardom of Catherine Deneuve*, ed. L. Downing and S. Harris, Manchester, Manchester University Press.

Azoury, Philippe (2007) 'Ozon, un "Angel" passe', *Libération*, 14 March.

Bonnaud, Frédéric (2001) *Les Inrockuptibles*, 324: 30–1.

Butler, Judith (1990) *Gender Trouble: Feminism and the Subversion of Identity*, New York, Routledge.

Hain, Mark (2007) 'Explicit ambiguity: sexual identity, Hitchcockian criticism, and the films of François Ozon', *Quarterly Review of Film and Video*, 24(3): 277–88.

Jousse, Thierry (1997) 'Sans toit ni loi', *Cahiers du cinéma*, 519: 66–7.

Lalanne, Jean-Marc (2002) 'Les Actrices', *Cahiers du cinéma*, 565: 82–3.

Marvier, Marie (2003) Interview with François Ozon, *Synopsis*, 25: 14–21.

Internet sources

Doustaly, Thomas (1999) *Têtu*, 37.

Guillomeau, Piéric and Thoret, Jean-Baptiste (1999) *Starfix*, 7, July/August, both from www.francois-ozon.com, accessed July 2007.

3

Shadow of the spectre: cinema beyond relation?

François Ozon's cinema experiments wildly, as we have seen, with both the representation of forms of sexuality and the representation of forms of power. Neither type of experimentation on its own generates lasting or significant change in the worlds of his protagonists, however, since Ozon's films gravitate towards the idea that a spectre beyond both sexuality and power haunts humans, that it is this spectre and its negotiation that will determine the capacity for relation between subjects, and perhaps even the capacity for life itself. On the other side of haunting by this spectre – a spectre which almost always takes the form of an alternately monstrous or insipid father figure – may lie, many of the films seem playfully to suggest, a fantastically cohesive, utterly reconstructed 'we', a blissfully united community quite beyond the neuroses of the patriarchal nuclear family. In the cases of both *Sitcom* and *8 femmes*, for example, this new group formation constitutes the film's final sequence, and the viewer is left simply wondering to what degree he or she can take seriously such a cinematic blueprint for a radically postmodern kinship. In both cases, the films' denouements reveal the variously over-feminised and hystericised family members no longer as superficial consumers of transgressive 'difference', or of desiring fantasy, but instead capable of absorbing their experience at a quasi-revolutionary psycho-social level, of emerging as a new collective beyond the father-fixated ideological terms from which it was previously composed.[1] In the final frames of

1 This post-revelatory 'positive' outcome can be claimed for many of Ozon's other films of the 1990s: *Victor, La Petite Mort, Une Rose entre nous, Une Robe d'été* and *Les Amants criminels* all offer their (male) protagonists an instance of horrific vision, an instance that is followed by a certain liberation from their spectral

both films – the funeral party of *Sitcom*, the dance of the eight women in *8 femmes* – the characters no longer posture as instantly recognisable deviant types, but instead exude a strangely calm, post-neurotic indifference to the norms of the social ritual in which they participate. This indifference appears precipitated in both cases by neither sexual play nor power play, then, but rather by the narrative's eventual pricking by a wholly unexpected climactic 'revelation'. The fantastical rat transformation in *Sitcom*, like the unmasking of the undead father in *8 femmes*, function as climaxes that push the various characters towards the brink of urgency and insight, and subsequently over into a somewhat improbable state of grace, capable at last of non-desiring communication, interaction and harmony.

The vast majority of Ozon's films in the 2000s, however, drastically reduce even a playful presentation of new relations constructed upon the ashes of a successfully conjured, revealed and exorcised spectral father. As Ozon's cinema develops, and in tandem with his generally increased budgets, popularity and acclaim, the likelihood of a given film's construction of a successful, post-revelatory 'togetherness' divested of these anxiety-inducing spectres becomes horribly slim. The films in Ozon's second decade of production are marked by a sharply increased cynicism, an altogether more solemn renunciation of the potential, no matter how ludic, for new forms of intimacy, kinship and community. Outbursts of violence and transformation seem to come earlier and earlier in the narrative, seem to operate less and less as cathartic end points of a revelatory struggle towards something beyond them. The films instead integrate this violence as their insidious and quotidian norm, and the characters, ever more listless and solipsistic, struggle with a barely perceptible spectre that hovers over them with a continuously despotic and ungraspable insistence. These later films all seem to take a fundamental assumption regarding the impossibility of fighting the spectre as their ideological point of departure. Refusing or unable to *touch* the various spectres structuring their desires, Ozon's second decade of protagonists tend to give up struggling against them. The spectres instead merely seep into every crack of the film's narrative and the protagonists' increasingly blank psyches, usually aborting all possibility of genuinely new relations among the living from the start. Ozon's latest films all seem

anxieties. This liberation gives them a chance, at least, for personal resolution and a potential connection to others.

relentlessly to repeat the solipsistic tone of his very early 10-minute Super-8 piece *Les Doigts dans le ventre* (1990) which follows a day in the life of a teenage bulimic: they are presided over by compulsive, lonely subjects who stuff themselves with empty desires, vomiting, running from the world, preferring the solidity of their own moribund fantasies to the stimulation of living others.

La femme et la mer: *Sous le sable* (2000)

Sous le sable was Ozon's first feature film to meet with an overwhelmingly positive reception from critics and audiences alike. Widely described as the first concrete sign that French cinema's *enfant terrible* was moving towards something like a 'maturity' of cinematic vision, the film caused much enthusiasm too for its devoted use of the English actress Charlotte Rampling, offering the (then) 55-year-old performer her first important role in decades, and initiating something of a renaissance in her career on both sides of the Channel (and, indeed, the Atlantic).[2] Ozon himself speaks of his desire to make a film in which he could display an older female body in a simultaneously erotic, attractive and realistic manner, and was drawn to Rampling as the ideal vehicle for such a project.[3] Chronologically sandwiched between the cruel and campy 1970s tack of *Gouttes d'eau sur pierres brûlantes* and the outrageously melodramatic 1950s excesses of *8 femmes*, the film marks Ozon's desire at this point in his career to work on a simple, sober narrative, stripped of the baroque elements for which he had started to become known (and to which he would immediately return, with a good deal more popular support this time). As he puts it: 'J'avais envie d'aller vers une certaine simplicité'

2 Where Rampling had spent most of the 1990s in small roles and television movies, the first decade of the new millennium has seen her starring in major film productions such as Laurent Cantet's *Vers le sud* and Dominik Moll's *Lemming* (both 2005), as well as in Ozon's other films *Swimming Pool* (2003) and *Angel* (2006).

3 The filming of Rampling's physique in *Sous le sable* (and, to a lesser extent, *Swimming Pool*) seems to have exerted a bewitching power over many critics. *Sight & Sound* devotes an interesting piece to the significance of Rampling as mature female sex symbol (Vincendeau, 2003), while an article in *The Observer* is driven, somewhat more rashly, to state that 'anyone who films Rampling's body with such sensitivity cannot be a misogynist' (Hoggard, 2003).

('I wanted to move towards a certain simplicity', 'Entretiens à propos de *Sous le sable*', Ozon official website).

According to Ozon, and repeated by him in almost every commentary he makes on the film, the project was inspired by a childhood memory. Aged about 9 or 10, Ozon had witnessed, while on holiday with his family in the south-western French region of Les Landes, a Dutch married couple plunged into sudden dissolution by the never-resolved disappearance of the husband while bathing in the sea. The sheer traumatic energy of the remembered event is channelled by Ozon into a film that develops many of his already-existing thematic preoccupations – solitude, neurosis, spectrality and the sea – while bleeding them of their more comedic or grotesque dimensions, and extending a fierce, non-ironic sympathy to the character at their midst. Slim, well-preserved, fifty-something English academic Marie (Rampling) and her taciturn, rather overweight, French husband Jean (Bruno Cremer) are driving down from Paris to their summer holiday home in Les Landes. They talk very little, but seem united enough in their silent practice of seemingly age-old routines. Once arrived at the farmhouse, he gathers wood while she prepares pasta (without any sauce); they share monosyllabic but good-natured views on the wine, and go to bed. At the seaside the next day, Marie (reminiscent of an earlier Ozonian Englishwoman in France: *Regarde la mer*'s Sasha) reads Balzac on the beach, while Jean goes for a dip. Alarmed at Jean's non-return after she wakes from her nap, Marie enters a state of acute panic, the camera circling her rapidly as she questions an insensitively nude couple whether they have seen Jean. Marie takes off for the police station, but despite efforts to help her to locate her husband, neither the lifeguards nor the police are able to help. Marie returns – suddenly, awfully alone – to the holiday home, but is plagued by creaking noises in the night and compelled to return to the murmuring, uncommunicative, nocturnal ocean, and stare out in anguish at its oblivion. The second half of the film returns us brusquely to Paris, the more controlled waters of the Seine being the subject of its first shot. Months have passed, and Marie seems to have entered a new phase of existence, a rupture marked visually as much by the different kind of film to which Ozon now switches – Super 16 rather than the previous 35 mm – as anything else.[4] At a dinner party

4 Apparently this switch of film type was caused by financial problems during the filming. The same money issues also led to a hiatus in production between the

thrown by her friend Amanda (Alexandra Stewart), Marie meets an attractive single man Vincent (Jacques Nolot), who seems attracted and fascinated by her, and offers to drive her home. Marie accepts the lift but angrily rejects his advances in the car, and hurries up to her apartment. She is lying alone on the sofa in the darkness when Jean unexpectedly comes in and sits by her side. The couple talk about the party Marie has just attended, and go to bed, Jean not sleeping but simply watching over Marie. The viewer is cast into some severe doubt as to how to interpret these scenes: has Jean returned to Marie unbeknownst to their social circle? Is he a ghost? Has Marie gone mad, these images of the restored Jean merely wishful hallucinations? The next morning Jean and Marie chat over breakfast (although he does not eat), before Marie leaves for her day of marking papers in the Métro, swimming and exercising at the gym, and professing to crowded lecture theatres on Virginia Woolf. After reading an extract from *The Waves* that appears to disturb her so much she has to stop the class early, Marie is approached by a student who asks her if she remembers him from Les Landes earlier that year when he, along with other lifeguards, tried to help her to locate Jean. Marie refuses to acknowledge any prior knowledge of the student, or even the fact that she has been to Les Landes. Increasingly, the film depicts her in scenes of a similar kind of denial of reality or communication: she refuses to heed Amanda's worries regarding her (we are slowly realising) demented insistence that Jean is alive; she refuses to listen to her old friend and financial adviser when he tells her that she is living beyond her means; she insists upon buying Jean an expensive tie even though her bank balance is dangerously low.

Only Vincent seems, potentially, to be equipped to draw Marie

---

two sections of the film but, as with the film type switch, the overall effect neatly reflects the temporal and modal shifts in the narrative: 'La première partie, en été, est une sorte de prologue, l'exposition d'un fait divers. Le film commence à prendre un autre envol ensuite, en hiver. Tout est alors très mental, les faits sont moins certains: on est dans la tête de Marie, dont le parcours est ambigu, moins déterminé, plus flou, plus fragile, c'est un terrain de sables mouvants' ('The first part, in the summer, is a sort of prologue, the setting up of a news story. Afterwards, the film begins to take a different flight path, in the winter. Then everything gets very mind-based, the facts are less certain: we're in Marie's head, and its movements are ambiguous, less determined, looser, more fragile, it's a terrain of shifting sands', Ozon, 'Entretiens à propos de *Sous le sable*, Ozon official website).

out of an immersion in a Jean-fixated solitude verging on fantasist, solipsistic madness. When he leaves a message on her answer machine she laughs in delight, only for Jean to return suddenly to ask her what is going on. Jean – or, rather, his hallucinated form – appears to be functioning for Marie as a self-imposed regulator of her desire, appearing before her not only as the embodiment of a corpulent comforter but also as that of a bulky law. The real stakes of Marie's life post-Jean – and of the entire film – seem to be unfolding: how will she resolve the tension between needing desperately to cling to the solitary fantasy of a watchful, dominant, immutable Jean and Vincent's invitation to discover new forms of intimacy and relation away from the realm of delusion? When she and Vincent do have sex together one afternoon in his apartment after he has come to pick her up at the university, the sequence comically and poignantly illustrates this conflict at the heart of Marie's desire. On the one hand, she laughs hysterically at Vincent mid-coitus, seeming to ridicule – and thus repel – him for his comparative light weight as he lies on top of her, on the other she appears genuinely to revel in a new-found erotic pleasure once they change positions so that she can sit astride him. The sequence is the film's most oddly effective and affecting, helped enormously by Nolot's performance, simultaneously warm and nervous, a combination visually signalled brilliantly by the violently quivering ashtray that lies on his shaking stomach as Vincent and Marie lie in bed talking after sex. When Marie returns home she finds a message from the police to the effect that what is almost certainly Jean's body has been found. At this point no apparition of Jean appears to Marie – it would seem that the combination of this news and her recent pleasure with Vincent may have chased away his returning form for good. The deep sadness exuded by the film and by Marie as its single dominant subjectivity – Rampling is in every single scene – lies in the fact that this 'exorcism' is not something that can be welcomed with relief, but is instead a liberation burdened by unbearable melancholy and rage. In the sequences that follow, we watch Marie sealed into a lonely urban depression, alone among the Parisian masses in McDonald's and the Métro, utterly incapable of enjoying the prospect of a new relationship with Vincent or any of the other possibilities a life without the fantasy of Jean might offer. When Vincent comes to her apartment to develop their romance, this time the encounter is marked by Marie's sarcasm, by her obvious desire to distance herself (she eats her pasta plain, but makes sauce for him) from his attempts at intimacy, and by a brief return from a calmly confident Jean, who watches Marie and Vincent as they have sex in the former marital bed. Vincent is presented as an unacceptable – since real – substitute for Jean, Nolot's smaller build occupying less of the frame when he sits in the position at the breakfast table previously occupied by Cremer, his upper body positively swamped by the tee-shirt previously worn by the bigger man. The film's final section finds Marie ultimately unwilling or unable to accept that Jean has drowned. Despite discovering that he had been taking anti-depressants and despite the police in Les Landes showing her the putrefying cadaver that has the exact same dental records as Jean and a proven genetic link with Jean's mother (Andrée Tainsy, with whom Rampling has one scene of blistering emotional violence), Marie insists that the watch discovered on this corpse could not possibly belong to Jean.[5] Clinging to this 'proof' that her husband, her rock, cannot have definitively departed, Marie returns to the beach where, weeping uncontrollably, she feels under the sand for something, anything. Spying a man in the distance she runs after him, but the shape seems to remain as far away from her as it was at the start of her chase.

Sous le sable constructs its simple narrative of haunting – supernatural or, more probably, psychotic – around its central character's inability to construct her own narrative of her husband's disappearance. Inhabiting the unbearable space left by an abandonment or bereavement that seemingly has no explanation, the excessive, traumatic thing that is Jean's 'ghost' seizes control of Marie's wounded psyche to a degree that renders her incapable of forging links with any other character in the film. The spectator too is dragged into a mournful, unstable world in which the potential for the creation of new, dynamic relations between living protagonists is snuffed out

5 Marie's horrific verbal duel with her mother-in-law is one of the finest scenes in the film, erupting like a sudden, angry wound in the otherwise fundamentally depressed texture. Both women clearly deluded as to the nature of their relation to the impenetrable mystery that is Jean, their capacity for cruelty towards one another seems limitless. Ozon's filming of Rampling and Tainsy is similarly harsh and intrusive: capturing Tainsy's aged and ravaged face in a series of shot-reverse-shots between her and Rampling, the two characters come to mirror one another's ugliness. As with the relentless shot-reverse-shot pattern of Tatiana's obscene dinner-table interrogation of Sasha in *Regarde la mer*, Ozon demonstrates his visual fascination with the potential sadism of dialogue.

from start to finish, only the dead or spectral Jean wielding any influence over the decisions and actions of our heroine Marie.[6] The film makes it clear fairly soon, of course, that Jean is to be interpreted not as a tangibly fantastical entity from beyond the grave and rather as an imaginary symptom of Marie's rapidly loosening grasp on reality. Ozon himself speaks about the film less as a meditation on actual ghosts and more as an inquiry into the quotidian effects of living with unbearable grief, the pain of which, he suggests, in the French DVD audio commentary, quite naturally pushes the subject into a form of madness. Considering the emotional terrain carved out by films about sudden bereavement such as Almodóvar's *All about my Mother* (1999), he set out to make his own (considerably more pessimistic, it must be said) cinematic vision of human response to the loved one's flight into oblivion (see 'Entretiens à propos de *Sous le sable*' on the Ozon official website). The film is truly remarkable, though, for the way in which it uses the central motif of Jean's disappearance and subsequent haunting to push into fresh territory the often-probed theme of the mutual ignorance, the fundamental misalignment that inevitably exists within any couple. The film's opening images of the apparently comfortable, intimate silence that cushions the everyday activities of the married couple, the casual representation of Jean and Marie's seeming lack of need to speak to one another as he drives, as she applies lipstick, as they both yawn and eat plain pasta together convey, at one level, a mysterious, romantic loveliness gluing conjoined individuals together in a shared space beyond words.[7] And

6 Ozon's cinema echoes much French literature (particularly by women writers) of the 1990s and 2000s in its preoccupation with the negative, stagnant effects of haunting on inexplicably bereaved or bereft protagonists: novelists like Linda Lê (born 1963), Marie NDiaye (born 1967) and Marie Darrieussecq (born 1969) frequently build their narratives around such maddening dynamics. This contemporary French vision of an oddly banal and fruitless haunting seems far removed from many Anglo-American equivalents. After all, whether in Shakespeare's *Hamlet*, popular film classics like *The Ghost and Mrs Muir* (1947) and *Truly, Madly, Deeply* (1991) or the influential television series *Six Feet Under* (2001–5), fictional ghosts often have the potential to be dynamic and dynamising interlocutors.

7 A film like Cédric Kahn's psychological thriller *Feux Rouges* (2004) – highly comparable to *Sous le sable* in its narrative premise of a middle-aged couple driving across France together for a brief spell away – could not be more different in its emphasis on the explicit articulation of discord and fragmentation within the couple.

yet, what that 'comfortable' silence dramatically gives way to in the film's second half is an unbearable silence, a silence manifested in the impossibility of Jean's ever explaining his disappearance, ever communicating a reason for his abrupt departure. Huge, impenetrable, yet also emanating an oddly familiar air – Bruno Cremer was chosen to play Jean not only for his build and manner, but also for the way in which his mainstream famousness (as Inspector Maigret) rendered him instantly recognisable to French viewers of the film – Jean functions as a colossal silent screen on which Marie's fantasies about a marriage sealed in harmony and togetherness can be projected. A flickering phantasm even when alive, it is hardly surprising that his fantasy-generated contours should remain in such keen operation after his death or its equivalent.[8] Marie's delight in cohabitation with a spectral husband, both pre- and post-disappearance, is merely the corollary of a subjectivity disposed far more to the machinations of its own fantasies and desires than to adaptation to the fantasies and desires of living others.

Ultimately, Sous le sable is the first of Ozon's works to address fully a question that in earlier films is evident only in recurrent snatches (consider the pre-Tatiana Sasha in Regarde la mer or Franz as houseboy in Gouttes d'eau sur pierres brûlantes): how to film the occasionally overwhelming loneliness of everyday existence? Marie's fundamental solitude swells monstrously as the film continues: this is no blip, but rather a form of being that ends up engulfing the entire cinematic experience. As Marie travels home on the Métro after a disastrous viewing of a potential new apartment (it looks out directly onto a cemetery), the intra-diegetic sound cuts out altogether and is replaced by the extra-diegetic strains of Chopin, the effect of which is to exclude the noises of real life, sealing Marie and the viewer instead into a private compartment. Marie's face is captured in close-up, head leaning against the train window (where it is reflected), worn out, absent; the subsequent shot shows her sitting in the underground Métro station, her expression again unreadable, apparently oblivious to the train that silently passes her. By the time we reach the film's final sequence, Marie's return to the beach on a grey winter's day, Ozon's

---

8 Cremer is often particularly effective playing characters simultaneously laconic and terrifying. As the scientist child killer Tessier in Jean-Claude Brisseau's much-ignored classic Un jeu brutal (1983), he once again straddles quotidian blandness and supernatural diabolism.

long (nearly 2-minute) close-up on Rampling's ravaged, weeping, desperate, shaking face takes the film-long exercise in the representation of solitary suffering to its emotional climax, and makes oddly understandable the character's ultimate compulsion to chase after the unpromisingly distant figure that lurks further down the beach. Ozon himself claims to offer no resolution to this enigmatic final scene, stating that he filmed it in a state of ignorance, certain only of the fact that he wanted to capture Marie's grief in a moment of uncontrollable, lonely tearfulness. As he puts it, perhaps somewhat disingenuously, in the French DVD audio commentary of the film: 'On ne saura jamais ... Pour moi c'est un homme au loin' ('We'll never know ... for me it's just a man in the distance'). If the image of *Sous le sable* that remains most firmly in the viewer's brain is that of Marie firmly and utterly alone, then, Ozon nevertheless does provide one crucial alternative image, a tenacious counterpoint to the representation of unremitting solitude, an indexical reminder that loneliness is but one living state of many in the universe. When Jean goes out to gather wood the first night that he and Marie spend in the holiday home, he lifts a rock, underneath which the camera shows, in close-up, an entire world of teeming ants, bustling together in the business of who knows what laborious or recreational community activities. The sudden shot of these insects is puzzling unless considered in the context of a film entirely concerned with the state of solitude. It seems to be included here in order to reveal, quite simply, that Marie, marooned as she is on an infuriatingly human island of her own creation, has nothing in common with these ants. Perhaps it is the glimpsing of this ant world, and the revelation of just how little it has in common with that of himself and Marie, that propels Jean towards his radical auto-evacuation.

Memoirs of a dutiful daughter: *Swimming Pool* (2003)

Swimming Pool was Ozon's first film after the huge international success of 2002's *8 femmes*, and as such was his most eagerly awaited film to date. With characteristic independence of vision, Ozon refused to deliver something to equal the previous film in glamour, wit or sheer bizarre excess. Instead, he opted for a return to the relatively small scale of *Sous le sable*, inviting that film's star Charlotte Rampling to join him again, this time playing an altogether less charming character, largely in English and stilted French, for a rather less dignified account of death and disappearance, dressed up in the predictably self-reflexive generic costume of a sex-and-murder mystery. From the opening shot of the Thames rather than the Seine, and the subsequent shots of Rampling on the London Underground instead of the Paris Métro, everything sets the film up as an Anglo-centric spin on the traits we have come to associate with Ozon's cinema. Interestingly, like *Sous le sable* and Marie, *Swimming Pool* and its fascinating central character Sarah Morton have inspired more than one specifically psychoanalytic investigation of the various behavioural tendencies Ozon chooses to explore. Ozon's panoply of neurotic heroes and heroines seems increasingly to appeal as much to the research interests of doctors and social scientists (Frankiel, 2002; Diamond, 2007; Schiller, 2005; Hesse *et al.*, 2005) as to those of cinephiles and francophiles.

Sarah Morton (Rampling) is a crotchety, highly successful, fifty-something British crime writer living in London with her aged father, and having a slightly frustrating affair with her distantly condescending publisher John (Charles Dance). At John's suggestion Sarah takes off to his country house in the south of France to work on her new novel, yet another in her popular 'Inspector Dorwell' series. Sarah is enjoying the solitude of her new, slightly exotic environment in the Lubéron when the house is unexpectedly invaded by Julie (Ludivine Sagnier), the pretty, vivacious and highly sexual French teenage daughter of John, about whose existence Sarah knew nothing. Furious, Sarah declares her refusal to have anything whatsoever to do with Julie, separating their food (though secretly pilfering Julie's wine and *foie gras*), leaving angry messages for the unreachable John and trying, unsuccessfully, to make headway with her new novel. Julie's exuberant personality and unrestrained activities infuriate the buttoned-up, apparently puritanical Sarah: she fumes – and yet cannot keep from watching or listening in voyeuristic fascination – as the young girl swims naked in the leaf-filled swimming pool or has loud sex at night with a succession of unattractive and uninterested older men. Julie appears also to be having some kind of sexual relationship with Franck (Jean-Marie Lamour), a local waiter with whom Sarah exchanges pleasant words on the occasions when she goes alone to the village café to devour profiteroles and drink tea. Sarah becomes increasingly fascinated by Julie and her unstable behaviour, eventually stealing her notebook, a pair of her knickers abandoned in the garden, and abandoning Inspector Dorwell to begin a new writing project, entitled simply 'Julie'. Noticing Julie depressed and with a black eye, Sarah invites her out to dinner, and the two women finally start to develop a relationship approaching intimacy. Julie talks of her first love aged 16 and of her French mother, a frustrated romantic novelist cruelly abandoned by John, darkly informing Sarah at one point that John is 'the king of orgies'. On a subsequent night when Sarah has stayed at home to write, Julie returns drunk with the waiter Franck, who recognises Sarah from the café. The trio share a joint of cannabis, dance together to some light techno, and Sarah returns to her room, where she writes furiously. Outside by the swimming pool, Julie and Franck begin to have sex, but the situation turns violent when Franck tries to leave, and Julie hurls a huge rock at him. The next day Sarah begins to suspect that Julie has murdered Franck, and starts her own investigation, in the process discovering (from a tiny, ageless woman who claims to be the gardener Marcel's daughter) that Julie's mother is apparently dead, from unspeakable circumstances. Confronting the increasingly hysterical Julie with the accusation of having murdered Franck, Sarah offers to help the girl to bury the body and cover her tracks. The two women toil all night burying the corpse in the garden, and Sarah throws old Marcel off the scent by having sex with him. Julie eventually sets off for a new job in Saint-Tropez, thanking Sarah before she leaves, and giving her her dead mother's unpublished romantic novel (a work, asserts Julie, in stark contrast to Sarah's own tales of blood and sex) to do whatever she wants with. Back in London, John tells Sarah that he is unimpressed with her new, uncharacteristically romantic manuscript entitled *Swimming Pool*, and tells her to go back to Inspector Dorwell. Sarah informs him that she has had the novel published elsewhere. The film's final frames show Sarah back in the house in France, waving from the window down at a girl by the pool who seems to be transforming between Julie and another girl, Julia, John's English daughter, of whom Sarah had previously snatched only a brief glimpse at the publisher's office. The sun shines brightly on the blue swimming-pool water.

In many ways, *Time Out*'s rather brusque appraisal of this, Ozon's sixth feature, is difficult to argue with: 'For all its many twists (which by the end probably become a little perplexing for the inattentive),

Ozon's film is predictable and derivative: why do blocked crime writers always fantasise themselves into a scenario which will restore creativity, and when is a swimming pool movie not about the return of the repressed?'.[9] Coming straight after the seemingly effortless panache of 2002's *8 femmes*, *Swimming Pool* to many felt oddly clunky, its huge sections of stiltedly delivered English dialogue (Ozon had his original French script, co-written with Emmanuèle Bernheim, translated) particularly grating at times. Trying to establish a definitive reading of the film is indeed a thankless task: Ozon's own rather bewildering mystification at the very idea that anybody might think there was a second, English daughter called Julia (Marvier, 2003: 20) is just one indication of just how self-involved a project this must have been for him.

Perhaps the two best ways of appreciating the film are, however, to focus on the often quite brilliantly comic detail in Rampling's playful performance (her deliberately hyper-English spoken French; her lustful guzzling of food and drink when alone; her zombified dance when acting stoned) and on the dimensions of the film which make it a flawed but fascinating addition to Ozon's many meditations on neurosis, solitude, fantasy and the impossibility of constructing relations with others. Sarah Morton comes across rather like a strange composite of *Regarde la mer*'s repressed Englishwoman Sasha and the same film's ghoulishly vampiric Tatiana. Saddled with the combined limitations of two such different types of women, it is small wonder that Sarah emerges as a character almost entirely defined by her incapacity for social intercourse. From the opening scene in the London Underground Sarah is framed, like so many Ozonian protagonists, physically surrounded by other bodies yet utterly alone. Revelling in her solitude and the assertion that only she is at liberty to recognise and identify herself, she rejects a delighted fan's acknowledgment and greeting, coldly refusing the woman's salutation with the declaration 'I'm not the person you think I am'. In the same way, she later declines all interaction with one of Julie's many ageing and semi-naked suitors in the Lubéron by simply pretending she cannot

9 Many French critics were equally unimpressed, the piece 'Eau plate' in the *Cahiers du cinéma* (Tesson, 2003: 48–9) offering a largely negative perspective on the film, accusing Ozon (rather unfairly) of only knowing how to make prologues and epilogues, and claiming that he uses fantasy as a lazy narrative prop.

understand French, thus opting out of any obligation to interact with the undesirable character. In the same way as Rampling's previous character for Ozon, Marie of *Sous le sable*, Sarah is, for all her anti-social misanthropy, thoroughly subjugated by her desire for acknowledgment by the distant, insipid, perennially unavailable 'father' that is her lover and publisher John (interaction with her actual father seems to have degenerated to the point of a vaguely fond mutual deafness). Those who actually reach out to touch her – the hapless fan, the successful writer Terry Jones (a sort of sibling rival), Julie herself – are, for the most part, savagely rebuffed, but these rejections take place, like those of Marie, within the context of her near-psychotic melancholia over an impossible relation with a patronising spectre.

On the surface of it, Sarah's gradual softening towards Julie, her fascination with the young girl's life, her mother and her seemingly chosen humiliations, appear to represent a major shift in Sarah's psyche, a step towards the desire to construct relations with a new subject that is neither self nor spectral father. The film would, in this case, signify a more optimistically community-driven project in comparison with the endless solipsism of the cinema represented by *Sous le sable*. And yet it is very difficult to defend such an appraisal of the film. For however we interpret Julie's ontological status – is she real or a fictional invention of Sarah? – the character is so relentlessly presented as eroticised, stylised and objectified fantasy *femme fatale*, Sagnier's body so constantly paraded before the gaze of Ozon's camera and Rampling's character, that she can only ever function as a conduit for Sarah's own desires. It is difficult to speak of genuine interaction between two characters when Julie is so resolutely used as a blank screen for Sarah's neurotic projections and narcissistic fantasies of transgression. However we interpret Julie's murder of Franck and the two women's collaboration in its covering up – is all this real or merely the substance of Sarah's new book? – this part of the narrative is really no more than a therapeutic and artistic journey for Sarah, one more project in the development of a 'blood and sex' intrigue, merely one that is conceived on her own terms, not those of John. Julie and her problems, real or not (and this really is a fruitless question to pursue), are no more than a ladder to be kicked away once Sarah has constructed the work that will allow her the twin prizes of a glorious professional independence and a smugly non-emotional indifference to the supercilious judgement of John. Sarah's triumphant published novel *Swimming Pool* may be a composite of her own consciousness and those (hallucinated or otherwise) of Julie and her mother, but this is no creation of a multi-subjective creature, unnameable and beyond individual identity, such as the one sketched out in, David Lynch's *Mulholland Drive* (2002), say, or in Robert Altman's wonderful *3 Women* (1977). True to Julie's injunction, Sarah 'steals' the story for herself, publishing it under her own famous name, and basking in the glory of a truly individualistic success. The final shots of her waving at a rapidly fluctuating, fundamentally ungraspable Julie/Julia from the window back in the Lubéron only reinforce the sense of Sarah as a solitary subject, forever at a distance from a companion who was always, in any case, never more than a flickering phantasm.

Husbands and wives: *5x2* (2004)

5x2 develops the keen interest in the minutiae of quotidian conjugality that Ozon displayed in earlier films such as *La Petite Mort* and *Gouttes d'eau sur pierres brûlantes*. The key difference here, of course, is that the union under scrutiny in this particular investigation is not that of two gay men but rather that of a married heterosexual woman and man. It is the essential 'normality' of Marion and Gilles's marital trajectory – its emblematic, 'state-of-the-nation' quality – that becomes of real sociological interest in *5x2*, making the relationship's violent and alienated failure all the more shocking and Ozon's cinematic vision of romantic love all the more bleak. This couple does not have the excuse of marginality or social disjunction for its breakdown: its steady corruption seems essential, predestined, an ineluctable decline into banal obscenity. Valeria Bruni-Tedeschi as Marion and Stéphane Freiss as Gilles (in roles originally offered to Sophie Marceau and Vincent Cassel but, let us be thankful, refused) were apparently cast as a result of the particularly promising chemistry they displayed together when reading excerpts of Bergman's landmark television drama *Scenes from a Marriage* (1973) for Ozon during screen tests, an episodic study of a relationship which *5x2* frequently calls to mind. Where Bergman's harrowing five-hour anthropology of married life enacts an almost blistering force upon the viewer by dint of its sheer emotional thoroughness and honesty, Ozon's film, like so many of his attempts to offer a new gloss on a classic model, occasionally lays itself open to the charge of a certain self-conscious and intertextual glibness. For all that, though, *5x2* is without a doubt one of the most brilliantly accomplished and oddly magical of all Ozon's features. Marion and Gilles's relationship is narrated with an important structural twist: their story is related in five discrete episodes that move backwards in time, from the couple's divorce day in February 2003 to the moment on holiday in Italy, a few years earlier, when their union began to take shape. *5x2* is far less contrived in its effect than Gaspar Noé's more jerkily shocking reverse-narrative *Irréversible* (2002): it glides gently and melancholically backwards with the ghostly grace of Cocteau's Orpheus and Eurydice. Ozon filmed his and Emmanuèle Bernheim's screenplay in backwards chronological time too, thus forcing the actors to share the spectator's experience of a journey from present despair to past hope, transforming the temporal reversal from what might have been just a post-shoot editing job to a veritable shared transfiguration of lived experience, an enchanted collective quest for the lost light of youth and hope. Bruni-Tedeschi and Freiss were obliged to lose weight, facial hair and wrinkles as the shoot progressed, literally shedding their older selves before the camera as they hurtle before our eyes towards a state of something like doomed innocence.

The first 'chapter', dominated by sombre dark-green colours and a reliance only on relatively limited sources of natural light, finds Marion and Gilles sitting in a lawyer's office, expressionless and jaded, listening to the words that decree their official divorce. After the deed is done the spectator watches, slightly puzzled, as the pair make their way together to a hotel room. Gradually we realise that they have come to have sex one last time. Despite Marion's slight embarrassment and hesitation, they begin the act, Ozon's camera capturing the plump, white contours of Bruni-Tedeschi's exposed flesh with an absolutely business-like candour. Suddenly we realise that the irreverence of the director is being matched by that of the male character. Gilles, despite the harrowing and loudly proclaimed resistance of his ex-wife, has decided to continue his brutal – and now clearly undesired – penetration, regardless. He turns Marion over and rapes her from behind as she screams in pain and humiliation, before eventually giving up her shrieks to silence. Gilles carries on thrusting towards his own solitary, grunting orgasm as the camera closes in on Marion's face, eyes wide open and filled with tears. Dressing in the hotel bathroom some minutes later Marion stares at her image in the mirror; returning to the bedroom she finds Gilles gone and the window wide open. He has not thrown himself out, however, but returns to the room in shorts and sweater to mock her for thinking he would kill himself over her. The divorced couple talk briefly and superficially about their lives, their present relationships, their son's school trip. As Marion prepares to leave, Gilles asks if she would be prepared for them to try again. She gives him a long, impenetrable stare, and exits the room, striding down the corridor to the incongruously, almost comically overblown, extra-diegetic strains of one of the film's many Paolo Conti numbers. Her face blank, Marion enters the lift, her reflection visible in the lift mirrors. The lift doors close. The subsequent four chapters each focus on a key moment from the period Marion and Gilles have spent together up until that point. The first of these finds them hosting a dinner party, presumably about a year previously, for Gilles's brother Christophe (Antoine Chappey) and Christophe's younger boyfriend Mathieu (Marc Ruchmann). The evening is a deeply ambivalent one: while there are moments of genuine tenderness displayed between the two brothers, and between Christophe, Mathieu and Marion, Marion and Gilles themselves seem utterly removed from anything like loving complicity. At one point in the evening, Gilles recounts to the assembled group a story of his own sexual infidelity: at a party-turned-orgy attended by the couple, Gilles had sex with random men and women, all before the gaze of Marion who sat in a corner alone. Christophe and Mathieu are surprised and fascinated by the confession; Marion merely stares into space, smoking, her eyes slightly moist, her feelings at Gilles's wilful decision to go on ahead without her (both within the action of the story and in his telling of it now) once again impenetrable. That night Gilles leaves the marital bedroom to go and check on his and Marion's infant son, with whom he sleeps for the rest of the night, leaving Marion to wake up alone. The following chapter takes us to the day on which Marion gives birth, and has at its heart the inexplicable inability or refusal of Gilles to be with his wife on this crucial day. The two characters do not share a scene during this chapter. Gilles receives telephone messages informing him that Marion has gone into labour, but he merely dawdles at his office and in the cafeteria, smokes outside the hospital, and makes small talk with his parents-in-law outside the hospital, eventually going to observe the tiny, premature baby in its incubator with Marion's

mother (Françoise Fabian), inexplicably reluctant to accept her affirmation that the baby she indicates is indeed his son. Later, Marion's
mother and father (Michael Lonsdale), he gruff and domineering, she
sad and resentful, argue with one another as they stand over Marion's
bed, making an already difficult day more stressful still. That night
Marion goes down to the incubators to look at her son, bathed in an
eerie, blue, hospital nightlight. Gilles, sitting in his car as it is being
washed, telephones her. The ensuing conversation is awkward, and
resolves none of the day's confusion, though Gilles does tell Marion
he loves her. She does not reply. The opening shot of the following
chapter reveals an ecstatic Marion and Gilles dressed in their wedding
clothes, about to take their vows. The reception is an apparently joyous
affair, the couple's wedding dance particularly rapturous. After the
reception, a drunken Marion and Gilles climb to their hotel bedroom
in eager anticipation of a night of passionate marital sex. As Marion
gets ready in the bathroom, however, Gilles falls asleep on the bed,
and proves impossible to wake up again. Marion puts on a pair of
jeans and wanders back out into the night on her own, glimpsing the
stragglers at the reception – her parents, Gilles's brother Christophe
and a young waiter – flirting their way through the end of the evening
to the strains of The Platters' rendition of 'Smoke Gets in Your Eyes'.
She comes to a clearing by a river, where a young, strapping American
man asks her for a cigarette before, somewhat forcefully, sweeping
her into a sexual encounter then and there. Some hours later, Marion
runs back to her hotel room in the dawn light, before covering the still
slumbering Gilles in kisses and cries of how much she loves him. The
final chapter takes us to an Italian holiday resort, where Marion is on
her own, while Gilles is on vacation with his rather sharp brunette
girlfriend of the time, Valérie (Géraldine Pailhas). The couple spend
much of their time observing and pitying the apparently desperate
singles around them, while Marion gets on with having a good time
on her own. One morning she swims directly into Gilles, who recognises her immediately as the secretary from his office. He invites her
to have lunch with him and Valérie, who finds her not threatening
but rather 'touchante'. We observe Gilles and Valérie's relationship
becoming more and more fraught as they play an angry game of
tennis and have sex that seems marked largely by Gilles's determination to dominate her. The next day Valérie sets off alone for an
organised hike. Marion and Gilles run into one another on the beach,

where they talk, flirt slightly, and venture into the sea together, as the sun sets magnificently and the credits begin to roll.

As this synopsis makes fairly clear, *5x2* is a film that is positively saturated in ambivalence and irony at every level: structural, psychological, aural and visual. The chronological trick of backwards narration, whereby the viewer knows of the horrors that will later befall Marion and Gilles even when beholding their most glorious romantic triumphs as a couple, renders sickly every image of contentment or apparent relational perfection that the film contains. Like ripe fruit injected with a nest of microscopic, disease-carrying worms, shots such as that of the final picture-postcard saunter of Marion and Gilles into the Italian sea, or that of the open, happy expressions of joy on the couple's face as they get married carry a disgusting undertaste. Despite Ozon's protestations – at the film's London premiere in 2005, for example – that the final sequence *is* romantic, a lush and non-cynical celebration of the couple's blossoming love within a present that knows no future sadness, it seems difficult to get rid of the sense that what the film really does is draw the viewer's attention, in a starkly distancing manner, to the fundamental mendacity of idealised images of joy when placed in a context of future suffering. The entire film is, after all, haunted by the early sequence of Marion's post-divorce rape by Gilles, a sequence that has occurred just ninety minutes before the blissful Italian sunset. What viewer is likely to have simply forgotten those images of humiliation and horror just because his or her attention is now being directed to the same couple's first stirrings of romance? The camera that shoots Marion and Gilles with such cool detachment from behind as they sit together, but not touching, on that Italian beach is no more a genuinely celebratory vector of loving union than the one that frames Marion, Gilles and their young son together in apparently calm familial harmony at the dinner table just minutes after the rape sequence: both shots are infused with the certain knowledge of the joyous image's repressed and obscene underside. *5x2* cuts relentlessly against all notions of plenitude, coherence and smoothly functioning progress. Images of contentment carry the virus of recently glimpsed degradation. Upbeat music such as the Paolo Conti track of the opening sequence or romantic music such as Philippe Rombi's beautiful score in the final sequence becomes sour in the context of radical failure in which it is inserted.

Fragmentation – of idealism, of continuity, of love, of the psyche itself – emerges as this film's supreme guiding principle. True to Lacan's famous dictum that 'il n'y a pas de rapport sexuel' (1975: 17), Marion and Gilles exemplify the fundamental schism at the heart of the sexual relation, the impossibility of a smoothly symbolisable, mutually signifying, coherent equation of desire between two human subjects. Whether in the unexpected rape of the opening section or in the comically premature sleep of Gilles on his and Marion's wedding night, sexual relations in the film are shown to be so many false, flawed and imperfect attempts to map a romantic or perfectionist fantasy of completeness or closure onto the unstable, fluctuating, ultimately 'lack-driven' situations and bodies of reality. The sequence in the fourth chapter in which Marion has sex on her wedding night with a handsome American stranger by the river has all the trappings of a fantasised, quasi-pornographic excursus, quite at odds with the realistic tone of the rest of the film. This disjunction sits perfectly well, though, with a Lacanian construction of romantic love within Marion and Gilles's married life. Like all desire, according to Lacan, it will be structured around a hallucinatory – and essentially masturbatory – fantasy produced by each partner individually, any semblance of real or spontaneous fusion within the pair (we think of Marion's sobbing cries of 'Je t'aime' as she rushes back to Gilles afterwards) utterly dependent upon the solitary fantasy for its illusory emergence. In the same way as their non-cohering desire, Marion and Gilles are equally impossible to grasp as characters, as flowing, meaningful subjects complete with understandable motivations and desires. The actors' ignorance of the development of their characters, forced as they were to film each sequence with no knowledge of where the next would take them, contributes to the viewer's overall impression that all he or she has to work with are five pieces of Marion and five pieces of Gilles, ten shards of subjective being that simply refuse to fit together, no matter how hard he, she or the actors themselves try to construct meaningful psychologies for these protagonists.[10] Marion

10 It is important to note the actors' confusion over aspects of psychology and narrative we might expect them to be sure about. Freiss, for example, speaks (in an interview about the film on the Ozon website) of labouring throughout filming under the misapprehension (or is it?) that the couple's failure is a result of Gilles's repressed homosexuality, while Bruni-Tedeschi speaks (on the French DVD audio commentary) of her conviction that the sequence with the American stranger is perfectly real (even though Ozon himself suggests it may well be a fantasy).

and Gilles instead remain mysteries or ciphers to us, to themselves and to each other. We all spend the film hunting for clues as to why they are doing the things they do, but are met instead by impenetrability and paradox, never by an overarching, cathartic or explicatory narrative or discourse. In Marion's case, it is the essential blankness and 'unreadability' of many of Bruni-Tedeschi's gazes that render the character so impossible to grasp as a totality. When she stares back at Gilles at the end of the first sequence after he pathetically asks her if they should try again, it is impossible to say what we see in her eyes. In the same way, those eyes appear simply glazed, slightly teary certainly, but fundamentally empty, during Gilles' orgy story at the dinner party. Later in the same episode, after smoking part of a joint, Marion shakes her head repeatedly, in response to nothing in particular: like a sort of mechanical ragdoll, she starts to emerge as a character we must be content merely to observe, but never fully to comprehend.[11] The character of Gilles is no less impenetrable and it is, in many ways, *his* inexplicable behaviour that functions as the film's central lacuna, a black hole of sorts, around which the various narrative fragments listlessly turn. The third chapter especially is constructed around Gilles' non-articulated refusal to go to see his wife and new baby in hospital. Throughout the sequence, we are blocked from understanding why Gilles dallies so, prevented from any kind of climax or resolution in which the character or some other mechanism in the film will explain his endless deferral. The episode instead merely imbricates Gilles's paternal function, from the outset, within a sort of unspeakable absence and anxiety, makes of him a silent, inscrutable, spectral father, perfectly in keeping with the more explicitly horrific Ozonian tradition. That this unresponsive daddy has the capacity to rape and humiliate in monstrous fashion elsewhere in the film's fabric makes Gilles merely an avatar of a more cartoonishly double-edged patriarch like Jean/Rat in *Sitcom*. What is clear is that whether Ozon is dealing us the fantastical farce of the earlier film or the sober drama of *5x2*, all relations in these films are haunted by the unexplained, ambivalent and fundamentally traumatic figure of the

11 Leo Bersani and Ulysse Dutoit's ambitious reading (2003) of Godard's filming of blankness, empty spaces and the fundamental absence of psychology in another film about the dissolution of marriage, *Le Mépris* (1963), could be fruitfully applied to many aspects of *5x2* (the number-based title of which also recalls other Godard films such as *One Plus One* and *Numéro Deux*).

fragmented father. In *5x2*, of course, and true to the lingering pessimism of this later cycle of Ozon's films, Gilles will *not* be killed, and his death will *not* usher in a cleansed community of loving subjects: Marion is quite mistaken, as he laughingly reminds her after the rape, to think he would fall from a hotel window for her. His puzzling spectre will, instead, remain troublingly intact.

More friends who didn't save my life: *Le Temps qui reste* (2005)

Ozon has spoken of *Le Temps qui reste*, which opened in France in November 2005, as a sort of sequel to *Sous le sable*, devoted entirely as it is to the exploration of its central character's struggle to come to terms with a sudden case of probable death, here precipitated by the protagonist's own diagnosis of terminal cancer. The Ozon film it even more immediately calls to mind, perhaps, is the 1995 short *La Petite Mort*, another tale of a belligerent, young, gay, male photographer, furiously shutting out the loving humans around him in favour of a self-destructive dance with something akin to oblivion. The film's sombre tracking of a dying misanthrope's last few weeks on earth is also more than a little reminiscent of the bleak 1963 Louis Malle film *Le Feu follet* (right down to its use of a resplendent Jeanne Moreau in cameo), episodically structured as it is around a series of essentially failed encounters between a rapidly expiring anti-hero and his various significant and insignificant others, both real and spectral. The narrative is straightforward: Romain (Melvil Poupaud) is a young, successful, attractive, highly-strung photographer who lives in Paris with his German boyfriend Sasha (Christian Sengewald). After a fainting spell during a fashion shoot, Romain is diagnosed with a terminal cancer which, even with immediate treatment, he has an almost zero chance of defeating. He opts for no treatment whatsoever, and resigns himself to death within a couple of months. The rest of the film charts a series of largely frustrating encounters between Romain and various other characters over the next few weeks, to almost all of whom he mentions nothing of his illness. At his parents' apartment with his sister (Louise-Anne Hippeau) and her small children, a cocaine-addled Romain verbally abuses his sister and precipitates her violent and tearful retaliation. When his father (Daniel Duval) drives him home, Romain provokes him by forcing him to stop so he can buy more drugs on a street corner. Father and son have a brief conversation about marriage and relationships that borders on intimacy and successful communication, but which is cut short by the father's discomfort when Romain kisses him. Back at his apartment, Romain snorts cocaine and has violent sex with Sasha, before coldly telling him to leave and that their relationship is over. Out at a sex club for gay men, Romain wanders into the backroom and watches a young man in a sling being fisted, both watcher and his object seeming lost in a kind of painful rapture. Romain drives to the house of his grandmother (Jeanne Moreau). On the way he stops at a service station, where he meets a slightly mysterious waitress (Valeria Bruni-Tedeschi) who engages him in friendly conversation. At his grandmother's, Romain at last opens up about his illness, telling the old woman that the only reason he has let her be privy to his secret is because she, like he, is near death. The grandmother talks about her many lovers, about her decision to abandon her son (Romain's father) after her husband died, and about her need to put her own happiness before that of her child, before holding a weeping Romain in her arms. The two go through albums full of old photographs and, later, unable to sleep, Romain climbs into bed with his naked grandmother. The next morning, the grandmother begs Romain to seek medical treatment for his cancer, but Romain gently refuses, takes her photograph, and drives away. Stopping at a service station again, he once more encounters the mysterious waitress from the outward journey, and this time she asks him if he would consider fathering a child for her and her husband. Romain declines the invitation, claiming that he does not like children. Romain's period of self-imposed isolation kicks off in earnest: refusing to answer the telephone he sits at home, increasingly thin, drinking alcohol, vomiting, and literally banging his head against the wall. He receives a letter from his sister, asking him to contact her so that they may have some kind of return to their childhood complicity. He can only respond by telephoning the sister as he watches her and her children in the park, stating simply that he is going through a bad patch. Only with his doctor does Romain enjoy a frank and quasi-intimate interaction, talking to the older man of the perplexing dreams in which he has sex with a vast array of characters: his parents, the doctor himself and his own childhood self. Visiting a church, Romain has a vision of himself as a young boy playing a prank (urinating in the holy water fountain) with a male childhood friend who then kisses him. The vision ushers in yet another apparition of Romain's childhood self, a ghostly personage who has popped up before Romain and the viewer from the start of the film: in the mirror at his parents' apartment, via a flashback of the young brother and sister playing in the forest near their grandmother's, and in another flashback of little Romain and his father discovering a dead rabbit. At the vision of the urination in the church, Romain weeps copiously, adding the stream of tears present to the stream of urine past, in a torrent of bodily seeping (at which Georges Bataille would be doubtless impressed). Romain talks with Sasha in a café and invites him back to the apartment where they stop short both of a totally honest conversation and of any sexual interaction. Back at the service station, Romain declares to the childless couple that he has changed his mind: the three have sex together, and Romain bequeaths his fortune to the unborn child. Increasingly skeletal, Romain shaves his head, and takes the train to a seaside town in Brittany. He throws away his ringing mobile phone and makes his way to the crowded beach. He takes a final dip in the ocean, swimming underwater, before crawling back onto the beach for a cigarette, where he lies as the holidaymakers around him gradually disperse, leaving him and his dying body utterly alone under the setting sun.

Le Temps qui reste is perhaps Ozon's least ostentatious film to date. Its stripped-down narrative, relatively sober soundtrack, understated performances and restrained colours all combine to situate it a long way indeed from the aesthetics of plenitude and excess that have so tended to mark Ozon's cinematic universe in one way or another. Every element of the film seems to function as a pallid, wan and wilting version of something that existed elsewhere in a brighter form. When we see Melvil Poupaud arrive on the beach in Brittany in the final sequence, he seems to be performing as the ghost of the strapping youth he played in Eric Rohmer's Brittany-set beach film drama, *Conte d'été* (1996), ten years previously. As Jany the waitress, we find Valeria Bruni-Tedeschi transformed from the dynamic and resplendent woman she played just a year previously in *5x2* into an unglamorous and slightly witless husk of a character. Even Jeanne Moreau, in a casting coup that predictably elicited much excitement around the film in France, pales in comparison with the highly analogous role – another flirtatious grandmother of a handsome, gay, ill grandson – played by Patachou in Ducastel and Martineau's excellent *Drôle de Félix* (2000).[12] *Le Temps qui reste* is perhaps the least seductive of all Ozon's essays on a given subject's brutally (self-) imposed non-intimacy with the living world. As a meditation on the imminence of death it is disappointingly superficial: various attempts to convey visual indices of its protagonist's proximity to annihilation – images of withered flowers, the heady confusion of the fainting spell – are especially jarring in their triteness. As an analysis of a passionately defended journey towards self-sufficiency, though, the film is intriguingly challenging. Romain quickly emerges as a protagonist with a fiercely defended impenetrability so pronounced as to make him as frustrating a hero for the viewer as he is intimidating a loved one for his friends and family in the film. Romain's relations with others in the film seem impossible to channel into anything as 'normal' as conventional friendship, love or kinship, mainly because they seem simultaneously over-intimate and alienated, 'too close' at the same time as being 'not close enough'. This is the phenomenon Ozon seems at pains to explore in this film, a disjunction as conducive to the central character's lonely, hallucinatory stasis as was Marie's unmanageable grief. The sequence in which Romain visits the sex club encapsulates the way in which the film dwells on states of simultaneously excessive and absent forms of intimacy, fusing the two apparent opposites into a disquietingly seamless montage. Here, Ozon's camera lingers voyeuristically on a sex act of radical closeness – the penetration of one man's anus by another's fist – all the while closing in on the expression of painful ecstasy manifest on the face of the passive partner. Extra-diegetic classical music of great emotional intensity wells up over the soundtrack as Romain watches the activity, embroiled in the two men's intercourse through his gaze alone, and yet as much a stranger to them as they presumably are to each other. The entire sequence conveys a bewildering mixture of fusion and separation, the sex-club setting containing a multitude of

12 This rapport between an adult gay man and an octogenarian older woman also makes us think of the much-documented relations between the late French writer Hervé Guibert (1955–91) and his great-aunt Suzanne. Ozon has spoken of his fondness for Guibert's famous autobiographical account of his illness with AIDS in *A l'ami qui ne m'a pas sauvé la vie* (1990), citing it as a far more apposite reference point for *Le Temps qui reste* than Cyril Collard's book and film *Les Nuits fauves* (1992), which (like *Drôle de Félix*) emphasises the desire for adventurous, communicative and singular life experiences which the subject's knowledge of his or her own serious illness can produce.

male bodies that, on the one hand, interact almost indiscriminately and, on the other hand, refuse the conventions of romantic intimacy with a radically isolationist defiance. This entrancing ambivalence sets the tone for the entire film, one in which, time and again, Ozon sets up situations in which Romain experiences his relation to others both with an overwhelming promiscuity and within a one-man desert. The film's final sequence, in which Romain lies pale, alone and dying, yet is flanked by bronzed fellow humans on all sides captures this phenomenon with a perfect poignancy, as does the shot that shows Romain in the foreground, smoking a cigarette, alone and on the edge of the bed, just after having had sex with the childless couple, while in the background the man and woman themselves recline in the bed together in tight, post-coital embrace.[13]

Le Temps qui reste offers its protagonist, weary of the living world and unwilling or unable to construct bonds therein, the phantom not of a former partner, but that of a former incarnation: the child Romain. The motif of Romain's haunting by the apparition of his boyhood self structures the entire film: the opening shot is of the child on the beach filmed from behind, the sea and horizon in the background, while the final sequence offers Romain the closest thing he gets to epiphany when the same child approaches him to get his ball back. The smile of recognition exchanged between child and dying adult would appear to signify some kind of acceptance on Romain's part for the person he was, for the child within himself, the attainment of a post-therapeutic self-love that should be distinguished from merely pathological narcissism. It is difficult, though, to get away from the idea of *Le Temps qui reste* as a film that is, in fact, suffused in a rather complicated and offputting form of solipsism, a cinematic vision that appears to have given up on all possibility of genuine connection across a community of subjects. Earlier Ozonian images of group harmony such as the reunited families at the end of *Sitcom* and *8 femmes*, or the finally amicable brother and sister at the end of *La Petite Mort*, seem to have been left well and truly in the dust. Ozon chooses instead to devote the entire film to the rapt

---

13 On other occasions Ozon very comically conveys the same dynamic of solitude within a putative 'group' through dreadful dance routines: we think of the sinister Tony Holiday 'Tanze Samba mit mir' routine *chez* Leopold in *Gouttes d'eau sur pierres brûlantes*, or the cringe-worthy gyrations to Whigfield's 'Saturday Night' in which Marion participates in *5x2*.

analysis of a single, inscrutable individual who, as played by Melvil
Poupaud, looks uncannily like Ozon himself, an individual whose
only fixation is, in his own turn, the rapt analysis of his own inscrutable younger self. As Romain and his grandmother peruse images of
their former selves in the photograph album at her home, and as she
pontificates about the necessity of putting herself before her child in
younger years, the viewer is left wondering what exactly the relentless
combination of discourses and imageries of a valiant and unapologetic selfhood actually adds up to. Certainly, the film as a whole seems
to lend credence to Anastasios Gaitandis' suggestion (2007: 10) that
'the *experience* [his emphasis] of narcissism [is] a seemingly unavoidable response to contemporary social relations'. It may feel to some
viewers like a cinematic celebration of an almost absurdly defiant
egocentrism.[14]

Misunderstood: *Un Lever de rideau* (2006)

Ozon's decision to make a 30-minute short film adaptation of Henry
de Montherlant's 1943 play *Un Incompris* came out of the practical
circumstances of the delays in the production of his feature *Angel*
(Rouyer, 2007: 25). A welcome return to what many feel to be
Ozon's artistic domain par excellence, the *court métrage*, the result
is a charming blend of archaism (of expression and sensibility) and
modernity (of costume and décor) that creates a beguiling aesthetic
disjunction reminiscent of his earlier adaptations of existing plays,
Gouttes d'eau sur pierres brûlantes and *8 femmes*. After the slightly
heavy-handed torpor of *Le Temps qui reste*, the piece displays a lightness of touch that recalls the earlier Ozonian three-hander *Une Robe*

14 Most reviews of the film – for the most part very positive – entirely ignore its
   potentially 'post-political' emphasis on the liberty of the narcissistic subject.
   When this dimension of the film is taken seriously, it can, of course, be
   interpreted in different ways. While Polo's reading (2006) is incandescent in
   its vitriolic condemnation of *Le Temps qui reste* as no less than a reactionary
   vessel of anti-socialist and anti-gay ideology, accusing Ozon of a 'vision morale
   et bourgeoise, saupoudré de machisme et de haine de soi' ('moralistic and
   bourgeois vision, sprinkled with machismo and self-hatred'), Fiona Handyside
   (2007b) finds within Romain's non-familial adaptation to his individual situation a highly progressive aesthetic 'in which the finality of death is read alongside the ever-changing interactions of both artistic and sexual practice'.

d'été. Where that film immerses the viewer in its ocean-framed and forest-edged exteriors, though, the world of *Un Lever de rideau* remains resolutely interior, its protagonist refusing, in line with most of the Ozonian heroes and heroines of this second decade in film production, to venture 'outside', as it were, to meet the other(s).

The plot is simple. Bruno (Louis Garrel) is waiting for his girlfriend Rosette to arrive at his flat for their date. Furious because she is, as always, late, he fumes to his friend Pierre (Mathieu Amalric) that he will break up with her if she arrives more than forty-five minutes after the agreed time of rendezvous. Pierre attempts to point out how unreasonable such intransigence is, but to no avail. As the deadline approaches, Bruno laments the fact that he will be losing a woman he really loves. The deadline crossed, Bruno goes to the bathroom to change, leaving Pierre with instructions to dismiss Rosette should she arrive. Rosette (Vahina Giocante) arrives fifty minutes late; when she explains to Pierre that she is late because she has been buying plums for Bruno, and will be going away with her family the next day for two months, Pierre drags Bruno out of the bathroom to see her, before leaving the two lovers alone to work things out. Bruno maintains his determination to end it with Rosette, but Rosette seduces him. After they have made love, Bruno repeats that the relationship is nevertheless terminated. Unable to believe her ears, Rosette pleads with him to reconsider, but Bruno stands firm: her chronic lateness is unforgivable, and he would not be respecting himself if he let the relation continue. Rosette leaves in tears, and Bruno holds his head in his hands, visibly distraught. Pierre comes back up, and tells Bruno how ridiculous his harshness will seem in a few hours' time. Bruno refuses to accept this, however, concluding only that they will have to wait and see.

The film is a perfectly formed, tragic–comic crystallisation of Ozon's increasingly consistent cinematic vision of the radical failure of relation between subjects in the face of a quasi-fundamentalist attachment to a spectral ideal of perfection on the part of one of the subjects. As was the case with Marie of *Sous le sable* and Romain of *Le Temps qui reste*, and as will subsequently be the case with the eponymous heroine of *Angel* (2006), the film refuses any kind of negative judgement vis-à-vis the protagonist's rigidity and, if anything, provides the viewer with as clear a window imaginable into a subjectivity that ultimately prefers its own rules, edicts and phantasms to the touch of others.[15] In casting the sulkily pretty and permanently pouting Louis Garrel as Bruno, Ozon provides the viewer with perhaps the ultimate embodiment of male narcissism in contemporary French cinema. Garrel – to a greater degree even than Melvil Poupaud – radiates a radically isolationist presence on-screen, separating himself off from the other two actors in every way imaginable. Where Amalric and Giocante seek him out with searching eyes, Garrel avoids their gaze. Where they articulate their lines clearly, Garrel swallows his half of the dialogue to the point that he is sometimes barely comprehensible. The three characters are split off from one another at every level: Rosette's bright-green dress, red scarf and little-girl pigtails contrast with the sober black-and-white attire of the two men; Amalric's short stature and hairy face distinguish him markedly from the slender, glabrous and statuesque figure cut by Garrel. As Valeria Giocante remarks with insight (in the interview dedicated to the film on the Ozon website), 'on a l'impression que tous les personnages jouent dans une pièce différente' ('one gets the feeling that all the characters are acting in a different play'): Bruno seems caught up in a Greek tragedy, Pierre is like the mischievous servant of a Molière farce, while Rosette appears to have wandered out of a film of the French New Wave. If the trio of two men and a woman recurs yet again in this Ozon film, it is quite without any of the pan-sexual potential we see the formation exuding, however fleetingly, in *Une Robe d'été*, or even in the dances of Sarah, Julie and Franck in *Swimming Pool* and Marion, Christophe and Mathieu in *5x2*. Rosette will shake Pierre's hand with disdain without even looking him in the face, and Bruno's apartment will become the space for separation, not union. Bruno is himself ripped into three separate shards, as the familiar Ozonian visual motif of his reflection in a three-way mirror reminds us. More, perhaps, though, than any of the other characters to have been reflected in Ozon's camera

15 It is worth considering many of Ozon's recent characters in the light of the writings of psychologist Dorothy Rowe. They offer continually lucid explorations of the fundamental opposition between the psychological types she refers to as 'introverts' – those for whom the greatest fear is their loss of control – and 'extraverts' – those for whom the greatest fear is being alone. The Ozonian protagonist belongs, almost without exception, to the former category: s/he is attached above all else to the world created and controlled within her own psyche. As Rowe (1994: 34) puts it, 'It is external reality which introverts find unreal. We (for I am one) look on external reality as being a passing phantasmagoria whose realness and regularity we have to take on trust'.

thus, Bruno is completely and utterly divided into conflicting and non-reconcilable sections of self. The shot of Bruno weeping, his head in his hands, once Rosette has left, is emblematic of Ozon's protagonists from *Sous le sable* onwards: alone as a result of their own attacks on others, they nevertheless lament their solitude with a pathos the camera can do no more than gaze dispassionately upon.

If *Un Lever de Rideau* definitely has the feel of a witty one-act-play, the pithy 'curtain-raiser' for the main event that would be Ozon's next film *Angel*, it is nonetheless as cruel an exercise in dashed hopes – for both viewer and characters – as anything else in the Ozonian œuvre. Altering Montherlant's play to make Bruno and Rosette actually have sex – and rapturous, romantic sex at that, the characters murmuring words of love, the camera dreamily circling above them – before Bruno drops her with as much force as ever, Ozon reinforces his increasing determination to pack whatever promise of happiness his camera may film with a bitter, nasty undercurrent, that will lash out as soon as the set of optimistic images has been released. Like the worm Bruno finds in the plum offered to him by Rosette, like the image of the dark and lonely sex-club backroom that supplants the picture-postcard shot of *Le Temps qui reste*'s Romain and Sasha in tender embrace, Rosette's sudden fall is as carefully orchestrated by Ozon as it is by Bruno. The film's final image contains, though, perhaps a modicum of hope: Bruno and Pierre together in medium-shot, share the frame, pondering Bruno's open-ended speculation about the future. They neither touch nor look at one another, but leave us, at least, with the infinitesimal visual potential of relations renewed.

References

Bersani, Leo and Dutoit, Ulysse (2004) *Forms of Being: Cinema, Aesthetics, Subjectivity*, London, British Film Institute.

Diamond, Diana (2007) 'Loss, Mourning and Desire in Midlife: François Ozon's *Under the Sand* and *Swimming Pool*' in Sabbadini, Andrea (ed.), *Projected Shadows: Psychoanalytic Reflections on the Representation of Loss in European Cinema*, London, Routledge.

Frankiel, Rita V., 'Sous le sable [Under the Sand] (2001)' *International Journal of Psychoanalysis*, 83(1): 313–17.

Gaitandis, Anastasios (ed., 2007), *Narcissism: A Critical Reader*, London, Karnac.

Handyside, Fiona (2007b) 'Alternative inheritances: re-thinking what adaptation might mean in François Ozon's *Le Temps qui reste* (2005)', *Literature Film Quarterly*, forthcoming.

Hesse, Morten *et al.* (2005) 'Rating of personality disorder features in popular movie characters', *BMC Psychiatry*, 5: 45.

Hoggard, Liz (2003) 'Vampire of the senses', *Observer*, 10 August.

Lacan, Jacques (1975) *Le Séminaire, Livre XX: Encore, 1972–1973*, Paris, Seuil.

Schiller, Britt-Marie, 'On the threshold of the creative imagination: *Swimming Pool* (2003)' *International Journal of Psychoanalysis*, 86: 557–66.

Tesson, Charles (2003) 'Eau plate', *Cahiers du cinéma*, 579: 48–9.

Rowe, Dorothy (1994) *Breaking the Bonds: Understanding Depression, Finding Freedom*, London, HarperCollins.

Vincendeau, Ginette (2003) 'Ageing cool', *Sight & Sound*, 13(9): 27–8.

Internet sources

Polo (2006) 'Every sperm is sacred: *Le Temps qui reste* ou le portrait réac d'un petit pédé bourgeois', www.melanine.org, accessed July 2007.

www.francois-ozon.com, accessed July 2007.

4

Blood, tears and song: genre and the shock of over-stimulation

François Ozon's early short film *Action Vérité* (1994) shows us four minutes in the lives of four young teenagers: two girls, Hélène (Farida Rahmatoullah) and Rose (Aylin Argun), and two boys, Rémy (Fabien Billet) and Paul (Adrien Pastor). The group are playing a game of 'Truth or Dare', all the interrogations or dares hinging, predictably enough, on issues of a sexual nature. Rose asks Paul if he has ever gone out with a girl. Paul dares Rémy to kiss Rose on the mouth. Rémy dares Hélène to French kiss Paul for ten seconds. Hélène dares Rose to lick her foot. Rose asks Hélène if she has ever slept with a boy. Rémy dares Hélène to fondle Paul's penis through his trousers. Hélène dares Rémy to touch tongues with Paul. All the questions are answered in the affirmative, and all the increasingly 'daring' dares are consented to (even if the last is met with a loudly proclaimed revulsion by Rémy). The four characters watch each other's replies and actions with a combination of embarrassment and acute excitement, Ozon's rapidly cutting camera catching their guffaws, reddening cheeks and bashful smirks in constant close-up. For the final dare, Rémy dares Rose to put her hand between Hélène's legs. The game and the giggles stop abruptly when she pulls out a blood-stained hand, on which the camera dwells in close-up, before a final shot of Hélène's wide-eyed, impenetrable face staring into the middle distance.

I start this final chapter, an overview of Ozon's cinema through the lens of genre, with that brief consideration of *Action Vérité* – Ozon's first film after leaving the FEMIS film school, a tiny project shot in a single weekend using non-professional actors, a small crew, and resembling nothing more than an amateur documentary film – since it provides an excellent illustration of the way in which

Ozon's cinematic narratives are so frequently invaded by an eruption of unexpected, arresting or destabilising visual, aural or emotional material at key junctures, an eruption which usually brings whatever frustratingly circular motion or deadlock in which characters and spectators have been spiralling to an abrupt end. Far from operating as a glib shock tactic designed to awaken interest and excitement on the part of an otherwise bored viewer, Ozon's frequently unexpected recourse to generic tricks and tropes such as suddenly gushing blood, tears or melodies may be understood as an attempt to inflict a far from gratuitous wound on the brain and senses of the spectator. Just as Ozon's protagonists must face being plunged into a state of sudden and unprecedented exception in order to pass to the 'other side' of their fears, neuroses, fantasies and desires, so his spectators must submit to an immersion, quite out of the blue, in aesthetic experience utterly out of the bounds of whatever they may have expected as conventional or consistent, in order to be jolted out of the inane stupor of a banal interaction with the film being viewed. Characters such as young Victor, the family in *Sitcom*, teenage Luc in *Les Amants criminels* or Sarah Morton in *Swimming Pool* effectively cross over from an increasingly tedious landscape of desire- and fantasy-based transgression to an outlandish register of what the psychoanalyst Lacan would term 'pulsion' ('drive'), in which their worlds and desires literally fall apart, and a monstrous mess of non-symbolic and non-identifiable parts is revealed.[1] If we turn to the procedure Ozon's films seem to perform via their spectators rather than their protagonists, we may find something rather similar taking place. When a film dares to violate its viewer by impinging itself upon the senses rather than the intellect, it usually achieves this violation through recourse to one of the so-called 'body' genres: horror, melodrama and pornography (Williams, 1995). These genres can be argued to be intrinsically corporeal in that they act directly upon the viewer's body, often forcing him or her to bypass judgement, reflection and analysis in favour of less voluntary responses, such as sweating, weeping or genital seeping. English-language film criticism, particularly in the

1 Neo-Lacanian philosophers such as Slavoj Žižek and Alenka Zupančič have proved particularly adept at reading texts and films structured around this psychoanalytic theory of the passage from desire to drive. See, for example, his analysis of David Lynch's *Lost Highway* (Žižek, 2000) or her reading of Laclos's *Les Liaisons dangereuses* (Zupančič, 2000).

wake of philosopher Gilles Deleuze's two groundbreaking volumes on cinema (Deleuze, 1983 and 1985), seems increasingly interested in the implications of films apparently worthy of 'serious' critical consideration which nevertheless simultaneously exploit the corporeal aesthetic typical of 'low' or 'trash' art. Steven Shaviro (1993) argues for a cinema capable of shattering the viewing subject's sense of self with the sheer excess of its sounds and images. It is, Shaviro suggests, only when 'we are no longer able to separate ourselves, no longer able to put things at the proper distance and turn them into objects' that the psychoanalytic paradigm of cinema as a kind of spell through which the viewing subject vainly attempts to cover up his or her primordial lack may be surpassed (Shaviro, 1993: 47). Shaviro is putting forward a case for the cinematic experience being more than an inevitable symptom and reinforcement of the human subject's allegedly constitutive fantasies, but rather a potentially unprecedented encounter from which the viewer emerges both shattered and transformed.[2] In much of Ozon's most startlingly original work, then, an abrupt aesthetic shift of gear is wedded to a psychic puncture or breakthrough in the narrative, with the result that the entire filmic experience is mimetic for both protagonist and spectator of nothing less than visually, psychically and physically experienced *revelation*. To return to *Action Vérité*, it is not the case that the sight and touch of Hélène's menstrual blood on Rose's hand is in any sense outside language, fundamentally obscene or the visual index of a putative 'monstrous-feminine' (Creed, 1993): the film's narrative and aesthetic 'jolting' effect does not emerge from any essentially mystical or abject quality we might wish to impute to menstrual blood. Rather more simply, *Action Vérité*'s final frames serve as a sharp slap in the face of the four protagonists, settling down as they were to an ever-more insipid framework for a teenage orgy, but equally as one in the face of the viewer perhaps him or herself settling down for a little underage titillation. Rose's bloodied hand, a conscious or unconscious development of the motif carved out in the early menstrual sequence of Brian de Palma's landmark film *Carrie* (1976), rips out the heart of the predictably constructed voyeuristic space shared by protagonists and

2 See also *Films, Cognition and Emotion* (Plantinga and Smith, 1999), for an apposite attempt to push traditionally psychoanalytically inflected film criticism towards a coming to terms with the potential creation of a hugeness of feeling in the spectator.

spectators alike, demanding the materialisation of a different kind of consciousness, as yet undefined.[3]

Throughout his career, Ozon uses tools borrowed from the toolbox of three genres – horror, melodrama and musical – in order to bring about 'hinge moments' of this kind for both characters and spectator. Interestingly, the trappings of pornography are generally not employed by Ozon in order to push his spectators towards a new dimension. Explicit sexual elements, while often present (as we have seen) in his films, belong more often than not to the blocked, circular or stagnant registers in which characters and spectators are trapped and seek to escape. Representations of sex are, in Ozon's cinema, often weirdly unworthy of comment: erect penises such as Stéphane Rideau's in *Sitcom* or Melvil Poupaud's in *Le Temps qui reste* are passed over by a curiously listless camera, as are the naked female bodies of Ludivine Sagnier in both *Gouttes d'eau sur pierres brûlantes* and *Swimming Pool* and Valeria Bruni-Tedeschi in *5x2*. Ozon's cinema turns instead, again and again, to the blood of horror, to the tears of melodrama and to the songs of musical to push his spectators towards an environment they really were not expecting, towards an improbable aesthetic register that truly does break with the terms of all that has preceded it. Not unlike *Sitcom*'s curiously fluctuating Cameroonian gym teacher Abdu, Ozonian viewers are often pricked in such a way that they may ultimately come to revel in the short, sharp bite of a rat's incisors rather than content themselves with a merely listless stroke of its fur.

3 In the notorious early sequence of *Carrie* in which the eponymous heroine played by Sissy Spacek finds her auto-erotic, post-volleyball shower interrupted by the unexpected onset of her first period, the intrusion of the girl's menstruation into the narrative register and the camera's close-up of the bloodied hand in the visual register both serve to halt the already established social regimes of play and 'safe' transgression in which the film's protagonists *and* spectators complacently dwell. De Palma's camera's comfortingly voyeuristic slow-motion cruise through a locker room of prancing teenage girls in various states of undress is brutally interrupted by a bodily function that is not in itself either abnormal, asocial or in any sense unrepresentable, but which gives rise to a horrific narrative development (the ritual humiliation of the protagonist by her classmates) that will both profoundly destabilise the intra-diegetic world of the characters and confuse, unsettle and interrogate any viewer who was settling down to a film that seemed to be pandering to the most basic locker-room fantasies.

Climactic repulsion: Ozon's uses of terror

French culture's relationship to the horror film has always been rather ambivalent. On the one hand, France was one of the first countries where serious intellectual discussion was devoted to the horror genre in international cinema. Film journals emerging in the 1950s and 1960s such as *Midi-Minuit, Fantastique* and *L'Écran fantastique* championed both American and British examples of intelligent horror cinema, enthusiastically locating the genre within the (somewhat more respectable) category of *le fantastique*, a category with deep roots in nineteenth-century French literary culture, and a precursor of sorts to twentieth-century surrealism.[4] On the other hand, French filmmakers themselves have traditionally been remarkably loath to venture into the realms of horror, intelligent or otherwise: nowhere in the history of French cinema does one find a director such as Hitchcock or Polanski, proudly and repeatedly associated with terror products. There have, of course, been 'one-off' French horror classics. Both Henri-Georges Clouzot's *Les Diaboliques* (1950) and Georges Franju's *Les Yeux sans visage* (1958) clearly set out to horrify, albeit in highly different ways: the former through the power of ghostly suggestion and psychological menace, the latter (extremely audaciously, given the era in which it was made) through its revelry in a constant atmosphere of entrapment and sheer bloody gore. It is to Franju that Ozon comes closest, perhaps, in his apparent ease, at least in the first decade of his career, with the flesh-and-guts directness of the Anglo-American pulp horror movie. While never setting out to make an out-and-out horror film, Ozon has repeatedly and unashamedly sprinkled his films, shorts and features with some of the trashiest, crudest and most generic elements of 'proper' horror cinema: fantastical metamorphoses one might expect to find in the world of David Cronenberg; zombies straight out of Romero's *Living Dead* films; dangerous psychopaths

4 If we compare French and American critical responses to the Jacques Tourneur–Val Lewton RKO cycle of horror films in the 1940s, for example (*Cat People, I Walked with a Zombie, The Leopard Man*), it immediately becomes obvious that while the French considered (and continue to consider) the series to be of crucial artistic, intellectual and ethical importance, for the Americans the films were merely superior B-movies. The reverence with which Truffaut and other directors of the New Wave approached Hitchcock also highlights the French capacity to find high art in cultural artefacts that superficially seemed designed simply to thrill.

who seem to have slipped from the country roads of a 1970s British thriller made for Hammer.[5]

While the often-made charge against horror aesthetics of this unrefined sort is that they are unforgivably crass, devoid of any mastery of what it really means to scare or unsettle the viewer through the powers of suggestion alone, it may be useful to consider their use by Ozon in a different light. All-out, gory horror at its most graphic can perform an extremely provocative function through its absolute revelry in the violation of the limits of the human body and the states that both characters and viewer usually take as unalterable. When Samantha Eggar's monstrous Nola triumphantly cries the immortal words 'Then look!' at the climax of David Cronenberg's *The Brood* (1979), thus commanding her disbelieving husband (and the queasy spectator) to gaze upon her revolting 'exo-womb' and the creature she is about to rip from it, she draws attention to the sheer outrageousness of the aesthetics being put on display for the camera, aesthetics that shove that spectator violently and unapologetically into a radically new register of experience, so new as to be experienced with simultaneous incredulity and nausea. Ozon makes careful use of such 'grossout' moments, inserting them at key junctures in certain of his films, with the effect that the viewer is knocked as violently into as horrifically new a space of sensory awareness as the characters themselves. In the early short *Victor* (1993), the eponymous hero appears to be haunted by a rigid set of unchanging and apparently unchangeable parental structures that seem set to last his entire life. But Ozon's brief use of unapologetically schlock aesthetics in one brief sequence effectively brings about the puncture of Victor's haunting by a fantastically embodied, literally moving appearance of monstrosity. Victor, in the middle of playing in bed with the parent cadavers as though they were a pair of giant dolls, manipulating their hands and genital areas in a frenzy of compulsive 'acting out', is – together with the terrified viewer – suddenly and quite unexpectedly *assaulted* by the momentarily revived mother and father. The parents, bug-eyed and

5 Ozon is, of course, not the only French director ever to have dared to import full-on horror aesthetics into his work. Jean Rollin's erotic films of the 1970s are unembarrassed in their utilisation of vampires, as is Claire Denis's hybrid art-gore cult classic *Trouble Every Day* (2001). Alexandre Aja's bizarrely compelling (if perversely reactionary) work *Haute Tension* (2005, released in English-speaking countries as *Switchblade Romance*) makes brilliantly bloody use of the *Hills Have Eyes* genre, featuring an unstoppably sadistic mass murderer.

filling the screen with their grey, dead-alive faces, jerk upwards to – at last! – castigate Victor for his inappropriate behaviour. For a few terrible seconds, the world established thus far in the film is turned upside down. A rapid montage of photographs of Victor as huge, grotesque, adult baby in his parents' arms flashes across the screen; infantile screams are heard from nowhere. The sheer horrific excess of the moment is paramount. The rising up in bed of the zombie parents, their arms outstretched, their dead, shouting voices ('QU'EST-CE QUE TU FAIS ENCORE, VICTOR?') crushingly, nauseatingly strident, is all somehow even more obscene and more preposterous than all that has gone before in a film which already contained more than its fair share of obscenity and preposterousness. But this aesthetic gear change is also wedded to a narrative–psychic breakthrough: Victor has at last, through a psychotic lurch towards the realm of the fantastic, been able to see and hear the hitherto still, silent, spectral parents as horrifying, angry, vengeful monsters. The moment is a truly disruptive one, both aesthetically and ethically, pushing both Victor and the spectator through into a new space, just as we were all, shockingly, getting used to the haunted space into which we had slipped. A similarly unexpected shift of emotional gear is enabled by horror in another short, *La Petite Mort*. In cutting out the uncannily staring eyes of his father in the photograph he has just taken of the (apparently sleeping) latter, then himself wearing the eyeless photograph as a kind of death mask, the protagonist Paul seems to be granted both new identity and new consciousness. It is worth lingering on the specific look and feel of the darkroom sequences in particular: yet again, we find that Ozon allies the ethical jolt exerted on his protagonist to the aesthetic jolt exerted on his spectator by the intrusion of a quasi-horror-film aesthetic. After Paul has taken the photographs of his sleeping/dying father we see him developing the prints in his darkroom in two separate – but similarly eerie – scenes, between which is sandwiched a bedroom dispute with his partner Martial. Ozon uses a dark red filter to bathe both these darkroom scenes in a blood-coloured light, while on the soundtrack we hear simply a low, droning, unidentifiable hum, over which is placed, at the climax of the second scene, a distinctly horror film-like heartbeat and a higher-pitched warning signal. These aesthetics stand in marked contrast to the mundane bedroom scene which comes between the two scenes, as well as to the humdrum vacuum-cleaning of Martial in the brightly lit living room scene that immediately follows it, marking the scenes out even more clearly as stylistic intruders, invaders from a outlandish genre, quite unexpected in the landscape of this family melodrama. The darkroom scenes present the emerging visage of the father in monstrous fashion. First, Ozon's camera lingers on the rapidly developing face within the print in close-up, the wide eyes staring out at the spectator and at Paul in terrifyingly unexpected belligerence. It is again in uncomfortable close-up that the camera films the eyes of this photographed phantom being cut out by Paul's incisive scissors, the ensuing shot–reverse–shot between eyeless photograph and Paul himself establishing a ghostly visual dialogue between living–present son and dying–absent father image. After Paul slowly puts the mask to his face, his own wide eyes staring out from behind the mutilated print (again in close-up), the next shot shows us the Paul–father in triplicate, apparently reflected in a triple mirror. The tripling effect takes the spectator still further away from the everyday world established in the rest of the film, and into the cinematic aesthetics of an enchantment or nightmare.

In Ozon's debut feature film *Sitcom*, the passage into full-blown schlock horror aesthetics, this time unable to be dismissed either as an alarming 'horror vision' (as could be argued for *Victor*) or merely 'atmospheric horror' (as could be suggested of the sequence just discussed from *La Petite Mort*), again coincides with the radical shift undergone by the film's philosophical internal logic. Just at the moment the protagonists undergo a veritable transformation of their psychic dispositions (and Jean of his body), the spectator is acted upon with alarming and unprecedented horror-film ferocity. The moment when the rat monster of *Sitcom* emerges functions in the film's fabric as a gash of radical excess, dramatically altering the terms and conditions of a haunting the characters have started to take for granted. The putative 'spell' under which the family have apparently been cast (and long since grown banal and predictable) is ruptured on-screen by something far more hard-hitting and (given the kind of narrative into which we have been lulled) aesthetically indigestible – a flesh-and-blood monster. Confronted with the lumpy contours of the hairy, flailing, sickeningly over-present, giant, raping rat, the unwitting spectator undergoes a puncture, an assault, a penetration that forces him or her simultaneously to laugh in outraged disbelief and retch at the sheer repulsiveness of the situation being depicted. The film's passage into a dimension of unapologetic metamorphosis horror occurs, we should note, immediately after the sequence in which Jean dreams that he massacres his entire family, along with Abdu and Maria, as they sing him 'Happy Birthday'. It is the supreme mark of the film's determination to propel the spectator onto an entirely new and unexpected plane of horrific experience that this *imaginary* massacre has been anticipated as an *actual* event, since the film started with a purely aural version of the bloodbath, before flashing back to relate the story in linear fashion, beginning with the day of Maria's employment. The spectator was ready, then, for an unpleasant yet credible climactic event. And yet the film narrative ultimately dismisses this 'realistic' (albeit gruesome) sequence as pure fantasy, and assaults the spectator instead into swallowing the reality of a truly 'impossible' phenomenon: a preposterously horrific on-screen metamorphosis. It is from this point and this point only that the family – and more specifically Sophie – can truly rise up in revulsion–revolt. In Ozon's follow-up feature *Les Amants criminels*, the 'new level', the space where haunting and neurotic addiction to transgression may potentially end, is inaugurated by the film's mid-way transformation into fairy tale and the arrival of the 'ogre' determined to make the teenage protagonists confront the horror of their murderous behaviour. Up until the point when Alice and Luc are shut up in the forest woodsman's cellar – with, we should note, the express purpose of being fattened up for eating – the spectator, along with the protagonists, has merely inhabited a narrative of teenage crime. After the film's plunge into the gloom of the forest, however, Ozon pushes us firmly and preposterously to a point where we must enter fully into the unapologetic fairy-tale horror of the situation: his camera unflinchingly shows us Saïd's rotting body, rats dancing over its limbs, while Alice declares, without a trace of irony, the improbable truth we must all now accept about the enormous, mysterious new character: 'C'est un ogre!'. It is here, in his decision to appeal to non-rational, quasi-magical, 'trauma-soaked' modes of representation that Ozon can at least start being compared with such French cinematic masters of the ethically progressive unreal as Alain Resnais and Jacques Rivette.[6] The hulking ogre, existing on the frontier of

6 Resnais and Rivette were arguably by far the most groundbreaking *auteurs* to emerge out of the New Wave period of French filmmaking, precisely because they dared, in a climate of relentless realism, to expose their characters and spectators to realms of experience so radically subjective as to be qualified as

everyday and fantastical realms, will confront the teenage couple with the unspeakable horror of the cycle of desire in which they have been previously caught. Where, in the 'realistic' world Alice and Luc have left behind, Luc and Saïd are radically different categories of boy, their perceived difference filtered through discourses invoking concepts of class, sex and race, in the ogre's fairy-tale world – the world that will become Luc's and ours – the two boys can be placed in exactly the same oneiric zone of exposure; they can literally bleed together. The absolutely irreconcilable nature of this new space of horror with the old, everyday, social space of the *lycée* is further underlined by the film's constant juxtapositions (facilitated by Alice's diary flashbacks) between the two contrasting environments. Furthermore, Ozon does everything possible to transform the woodsman, played by the Serbian actor Miki Manojlovic, into a figure of fantastical externality, firmly not of the 'normal' French world which allows and absorbs such casual acts as the slaying of Saïd. The actor's hugeness and bulk is insisted upon by a camera that lingers over his frame both clothed and naked; his foreign accent transforms him – within the inevitably xenophobic unconscious to which Ozon clearly appeals – into a terrifying figure of threat; his beard and body hair set him in a different mode of masculinity from the smooth, youthful, boyish likes of Luc and Saïd. The fantasy–horror represented by this ogre is one which, when accepted as such and in an absolutely non-ironic fashion, will come to 'unblock' the virginal Luc and precipitate him into a state of action. As with Victor's zombies, Paul's photographically spectral father and the *Sitcom* family's monster rat, the overwhelming force of the fairy-tale ogre is, in *Les Amants criminels*, ultimately experienced by the haunted or terrorised protagonist as a therapeutic force.

There are two important exceptions in Ozon's œuvre to the theory of a terror that might in some sense positively transform the protagonist. In *Regarde la mer*, the film's descent into unapologetic gore is simply too brusque to heal either protagonist or spectator. Both are instead

psychotic or fantastical. Ozon's cinematic dreamscape is no *L'Année dernière à Marienbad* (Resnais), nor even a *Céline et Julie vont en bateau* (Rivette): both these films display, despite their playful sheen, an earnest investment in the question of deranged and non-eroticised helplessness that is quite foreign to the impish Ozon. All the same, his aesthetic path strays sufficiently from the vast majority of his realist contemporaries for him to be considered, like them, and like his French contemporary Lucile Hadzihalilovic (*Innocence*, 2004), a legitimate child of Cocteau.

simply engulfed by the horror-strewn havoc wrought by Marina de Van's Tatiana. Fairly early on, the film offers a clue that Tatiana brings with her forms of repulsiveness that are simply impossible to integrate, shapes of disgust that do not inspire either breakdown or reaction, simply repulsion. When she leaves her excrement in Sasha's toilet and dips Sasha's toothbrush in the bowl of faeces, the viewer is seized by a sensation of simultaneous anxiety and nausea with regard both to the offensive character and the objectionable film in which she and her shit assault Sasha and us. Ozon's quite unexpected close-up shot of the thick and copious human waste in the toilet was deemed by the vast majority of the film's French reviewers simply beyond the pale, a crass and unforgivable violation of the innocent spectator's sensibility. The shot might be viewed as a metonym for the film's immersion in a horrific gratuitousness that – much in the style of the anus-driven values of Sade – refuses to be in any way admirable, productive or useful.[7] The shot is a precursor to the penultimate sequence's equally Sadeian images of Sasha's trussed-up dead body in Tatiana's tent, genitalia appearing (though the shots are too darkly lit and too rapidly cut to be sure) to have been somehow stitched, scissors and thread lying on the ground nearby. This denouement of utter horror is one from which Sasha the protagonist can in no way benefit, and one out of which the spectator emerges merely sickened. The film's final shots of a beautifully sparkling sea conveying the monstrous Tatiana to a realm of impunity, Sasha's mewling baby in her arms, seem to mock both Sasha and the spectator for ever dreaming that they might achieve some kind of romantic transcendence via exposure to a survivable horror. In the later film *Sous le sable*, Ozon seems to promise the protagonist Marie an encounter with an abominable representation of horror, the vision of a ghoul that will shake her out of our torpor and allow her, finally, to leave the tedious spectre of the disappeared Jean behind. But where, for Sasha in *Regarde la mer*, the horrific encounter will fatally overwhelm her, for Marie, it – and the aesthetic Ozon uses to represent it – will merely 'underwhelm', and thus fail to provide

7 Mark Hain (2007: 282) suggests that with their occasional overgraphic moments Ozon and Hitchcock 'dredged up more of the darkness lurking beneath the surface than we wanted to see; what was titillating in its hidden-ness now confronts us, and our sadistic pleasures profoundly disturb us. It's as if we've been betrayed – not simply by the directors, but by the limits of our own capacity to justify our voyeuristic thrills'.

effective therapy. In the scene at the morgue towards the end of the film we, like Marie, brace ourselves for the sight of Jean's stinking, rotting, unrecognisable cadaver, but instead of revealing it to us (in the manner of the rat monster, the ogre, the zombie parents, etc.) Ozon's camera remains on Rampling's face, capturing her sharp intake of breath, her ever-widening eyes, but refusing to allow the viewer to share this experience. An image of true *schlock* horror is thus occluded from *Sous le sable*'s 'tasteful' aesthetic. It hardly comes as a surprise, given what we have established regarding the importance of the horrific 'puncture' for the 'unblocking' of the narrative deadlock, when Marie subsequently refuses the truth of what she has only apparently seen, insists that the corpse is not Jean, and continues her self-imposed delusional haunting. The corollary of the absence of over-present horror is, or so it would seem, the triumph of psychic stagnation.

'If I Only Had a Heart!': Ozon, the social body and the knowing musical

When the European musical film takes cues from its Hollywood precursors, it is usually to the internally fragmented, self-reflexive and somehow *fraught* mode of, say, Vincente Minnelli, that it tends to turn when using its song-and-dance routines to paint the relations of its characters. Some critics (their arguments outlined in Cook and Bernink, 1999: 210) have suggested that the social, psychological, existential and political struggles of Minnelli's characters emerge precisely through the often ambivalent musical numbers in which they perform. France's musical film director par excellence Jacques Demy, a director Ozon cites as a key aesthetic influence on *8 femmes* (but whose bittersweet general sensibility in fact filters down – albeit in crueller form – to much of Ozon's other work) serves as an excellent example of the way in which the modern European musical so often uses its song-and-dance routines to present social fracture in new terms. A number like 'Marins, Amis, Amants ou Maris' in Demy's 1966 film *Les Demoiselles de Rochefort* serves to underline the fundamental schism at the heart of the Étienne–Bill–Esther–Judith quartet, a pseudo-romantic formation that will crumble soon after the song's performance. As for the Lilac Fairy (Delphine Seyrig)'s sung advice to the unfortunate Princess (Catherine Deneuve), sexually pursued by her father the King (Jean Marais) in Demy's fairytale musical *Peau d'âne* (1970), its musically articulated dissuasion from incest underlines with obscene levity the horror lurking beneath the royal family's model for social, romantic and familial cohesion in this particular universe. Demy often uses musical sequences to point, then, to an ironic disjunction within the social body performing in these sequences. Elsewhere, Demy oscillates wildly between musical set pieces that seem to confirm social and familial unity with such self-consciously performative panache that the final effect could be interpreted as parody, and musical sequences that exist as sheer, desperate, out-of-control 'punctures', painful dents in the fabric of the film, musical moments that signal experiences of emotion so overwhelming, so unmanageable, that their subjects are somehow ejected from social functioning, and teeter close to hysterical break-down. A famous example of the former – 'over-performed' closeness as it were – is the smug and bouncy 'Nous sommes deux sœurs jumelles' routine performed by Solange (Françoise Dorléac) and Delphine (Catherine Deneuve) in *Les Demoiselles de Rochefort*, the sisters' chorus of unity (complete with trumpets) almost smothering the overwhelmed viewer so close to the start of the film. In 1964's *Les Parapluies de Cherbourg*, however, the film's central musical piece, and the only conventional song to be performed throughout the entire film, conveys the almost unbearably painful separation of Guy (Nino Castelnuevo) and Geneviève (Catherine Deneuve) when Guy is called up for military service in Algeria: here, then, full-blown musical performance emerges in tandem with romantic experience so intense that the couple itself is obliterated.[8] Like Demy, Ozon's use of song in his films seems to veer between three basic positions: first, the song as a kind of illustrative dance, starkly explicating the tension within the group performing, second, the song as an over-the-top exercise in an orchestrated collective identity so tenuous as to appear either

8 Similarly, in Alain Resnais's *Muriel ou le temps d'un retour* (1963), the song 'Déjà', unexpectedly performed (for this is no musical) by the avenging angel character of Ernest towards the end of the film, serves to explode the diseased social group that has been in operation for the majority of the film. Lars von Trier's use of highly emotional musical performances by Björk in the singular musical melodrama *Dancer in the Dark* (2001) is equally disruptive, the songs cutting through oppressive 'legal' practices of factory labour and capital punishment like piercing grenades.

dangerously provisional or else ridiculous, and, third, the song as an intrusion of highly emotional musicality so intense that it threatens to overwhelm the character embroiled in the piece, throw the character further still outside the group in which she or he seeks to fit, and 'puncture' the controlled sensibilities hitherto displayed within the film in such a way that neither character nor spectator fully recovers.

The opening song-and-dance sequence of the short film *Une Robe d'été* (1996) illustrates with a wonderfully comedic knowingness the possibilities of the socially explicatory dance. The sequence is intra-diegetic, that is, inserted into the narrative itself, and it is performed in a realistic (or, at least, semi-realistic) context, the music having an identifiable and feasible source located within the world of the film, with the characters acknowledging (to a certain degree) the exception-ality of musical performance within an everyday setting. Sébastien gleefully dances and mimes the Sheila song 'Bang Bang' (the tape of which he has set off with a determined press of the toe) in his tight swimming trunks, while his boyfriend Luc squirms in embar-rassment at the sheer campness of it all, before getting dressed and taking off on his bicycle, abruptly cutting the performance short as the camera follows him out on the road rather than remaining in the musical world of Sébastien. The musical sequence serves to operate as a starkly hilarious revelation of the fundamental clash between the opposed worlds of the two men as things stand at the start of the film: Luc's aggressive, naturalised, practical 'masculinity' (he busies himself with the serious business of getting dressed, angrily avoiding the gaze of either the camera or his boyfriend) versus Sébastien's saccharine, staged, 'effeminate' revelry in the delights of the song (he stares seductively into the camera and at Luc, moving his body in time with the music with all the careful planning of Monroe). The two characters would appear to inhabit different film genres altogether: one is delighted to be the star of a musical of his own design, while the other cannot wait to leave for the 'real' world of the beach (and, subse-quently, heterosexuality). The visual, musical and gestural argument between the characters over whether or not they are in a musical presided over by the pop icon of French camp that is Sheila, is precisely what illustrates the antagonism between them, an antagonism that will be smoothed out to some extent not only by the increasing fluidity of the distribution of sexual roles in the film (discussed in Chapter 1), but also by the return of Sheila's song in the final frames of the film, this time occurring extra-diegetically, over the image of Luc's relaxed and happy face. Ozon returns with his most determined zeal to the socially illustrative possibilities of song and dance with his one 'true' musical, *8 femmes* (2002). In this film, the musical sequences remain intra-diegetically woven into the narrative, all the characters acknowledging the intrusion of the performance as intrusion, but the realism of the tape recorder been abandoned in favour of eight non-explained sources of musical accompaniment and backing. Three performances in particular operate with a powerfully explicatory power, all placing the performer in the position of manipulator, oppressor and seductress of her rapt audience. First, Catherine/Ludivine Sagnier's rendition of another Sheila song 'Papa, t'es plus dans le coup', sung in her pyjamas, cheekily silences her nagging grandmother and peevish aunt, and establishes her once and for all as the vibrant, rebellious and anti-authoritarian figure of the piece, a (false) position she will use to conceal her, in fact, highly conservative collaboration with the silent Papa. The film's opening song, then, far from being the innocuous piece of fluff it at first appears to the bemused spectator, establishes in powerful musical terms some of the central relational dynamics of the film. Throughout the number, Sagnier looks with wide eyes into the camera, dances with an almost manically youthful energy, and spontaneously enlists her mother and sister as backing singers: all are postures that operate simultaneously as mere choreographic details and as deeply significant narrative signposts. In the same way, Pierrette/Fanny Ardant's and Louise/Emmanuelle Béart's highly eroticised performances of (respectively) the slinky 'A quoi sert de vivre libre?' and the frenetic 1980s French pop hit 'Pile ou face' function as bullying seductions of the other women that watch them. Both characters take up a position at the centre of the frame (or stage), from which they pout, leer and disrobe (Pierrette) or let their hair down (Louise) for the less confident women watching. While Pierrette's Gilda-esque shimmies seem directed at all seven women rivals (even if the gazes of the two women over whom she enjoys sexual conquest at some point in the narrative, Mme Chanel and Gaby, are most beadily observed by Ozon's camera, equally interested in the intra-diegetic audience and the performer) Louise focuses single-mindedly on the awkwardly 'un-feminine' spectator Augustine/Isabelle Huppert. Béart's Madonna-esque gyrations aggressively assert Louise's rights – as a good performer – to a higher ranking on the scale of womanliness. Knowing how to perform impressively in one's ascribed musical number is, in this film, then, not a mere question of detail: it is inextricably linked to one's acceptability as a gendered being. The song-and-dance routine is, in Ozon, a question of sexual politics. Perhaps the single most arresting instance of the Ozonian 'socio-political' dance, disturbing and hilarious in equal measure, is the performance *à quatre* of 'Tanze Samba mit mir' set in motion by the terrifying Daddy-figure Leopold midway through *Gouttes d'eau sur pierres brûlantes* (2000). Here, as in *Une Robe d'été*, an intra-diegetic record (a 1970s German pop hit sung by Tony Holiday) is (semi-realistically) set spinning by a character keen to inhabit a film musical of which he is both choreographer and star dancer, but unlike the ineffectual Sébastien in his swimming trunks, Leopold, dressed in fashionable slacks and a sweater that clings to his big chest, effortlessly commandeers his three weaker companions – Vera in miniskirt and high boots, Anna in bra and panties, and Franz in sensible short-sleeved shirt and trousers – into joining in the performance, no questions asked. The four characters segue without a murmur into a regimented dance, as though the apartment had magically been converted into a discotheque. Leopold stares confidently straight ahead at an unspecified point beyond the camera as he dances, moving his arms and swivelling his hips, Anna giggles and simpers her way through the performance, watching Leopold for guidance, while Vera summons up her natural cool to bring off a creditable set of moves. Only Franz seems utterly at a loss throughout the impromptu performance, coming in late with his handshaking movements, jumping around at the wrong moment, and looking anxiously at the other three for any morsel of choreographic advice they might have to offer. The dance sequence crystallises the wider dynamic taking place among the characters in absurd musical terms, trapping them in their preordained roles more tightly than ever. Once Leopold claps his hands to signify the end of the dance and the beginning of the orgy at which he will preside, the performers will never shake themselves free of the political positions the dance has sealed them into: Leopold as commandant, Anna and Vera as more or less successful collaborators, and Franz as helplessly unfashionable detritus.

Dance sequences such as these highlight the tensions and imbalances inherent in the groups that perform, but elsewhere Ozon does appear to use musical performances to establish a kind of newfound harmony within a group. The problem with these instances of near-utopian fusion, however, is that within them Ozon usually plants an unstable, excessive or otherwise somehow ambivalent aspect that threatens to tip the characters involved in the musical sequence in question into a state of imminent dissolution. Thus, in *8 femmes*, Augustine/Isabelle Huppert manages, by dint of her seated, majestic, piano-accompanied performance of Françoise Hardy's 'Message personnel', to gain the attention and respect of some of her fellow women, even coaxing Mme Chanel, Mamy, Suzon and Catherine into singing backing vocals and swaying in sympathy. For a moment, the acrimony of the preceding scene is forgotten, and the musical performance appears to have ushered in a new state of calm and unity. This is instantly shattered, though, once the song is over, Augustine puts her glasses back on, and the characters who have been outside during the performance return. Fragmentation, discord and unsung words return, the peace of the musical sequence dissolved. An ambivalent effect is created too by Mamy/Danielle Darrieux's rendition of George Brassens's 'Il n'y a pas d'amour heureux'. A performance that appears to unite all eight women in a tranquil and generous new formation of dancing couples is nevertheless marred, tinged with a drop of inevitable heartache, by the simple fact of the words of the song – 'Il n'y a pas d'amour heureux' ('There is no happy love') could not offer a more pessimistic account of the impossibility of fruitful and rewarding bonds between individuals, and Darrieux's mournful musical utterance of this poem of lifelong, isolated frustration seems, rather like an equivalent to the rat crawling across the gravestone just when the *Sitcom* family appears to have been reborn as a new unit, to pour cold, ironic water on the new relations we see evolving through dance. Whenever, then, Ozon presents a musical dance sequence that does apparently seal its performers into warmth, intimacy and new possibilities of unforeseen loving interaction, he quickly injects some conflicting, contextually ironic or disrupting element to compromise its aesthetically cohesive action. *Swimming Pool*'s Sarah, Julie and Franck sway sensually (although, in the case of Rampling's stiff but stoned Sarah, the effect is deeply comical) to Steve Everitt's dance track 'Mirror-ball', the combination of music and motion providing an unexpected source of triangular eroticism, just as *5x2*'s Marion, her brother-in-law Christophe and his boyfriend Mathieu create, in their wonderfully spontaneous dance of Paolo Conti's Italian ballad 'Sparring Partner', a sequence of powerfully emotional and sexual power. In both films, the 2-minute sequences of a trio of suddenly – this time extremely realistically – dancing characters becoming absorbed in each other, marijuana and the music being played in the background quickly give way to, in the latter case, images of solitude and melancholia and, in the former, murder and madness. *5x2* in particular seems to revel in sequences of beautifully romantic music which are – in an oddly sadistic way – undercut by their context. The post-wedding reception stragglers – Marion's parents – are framed in quite aurally and visually idealised bliss as they dance to the Platters' rendition of 'Smoke Gets in Your Eyes', yet throughout the heart-warming sequence (which we see through Marion's eyes) we remain aware of the far from romantic reality of the older couple, a future reality we have already witnessed in the previous chapter of the backwards-narrated film. The dance sequence here brings the couple together in a moment of togetherness that seems – the film appears to imply – able to last only the length of the song. As for Gilles and Marion's own wedding dance, Ozon strives to create an effect of unprecedented romanticism (strikingly reminiscent of the wondrous fairground sequence in Jacques Demy's 1960 masterpiece *Lola*): the intra-diegetic music cuts out, Philippe Rombi's extra-diegetic score dominating the soundtrack instead, slow motion sets in, and the entire sequence is invaded by a resplendent light. Valeria Bruni-Tedeschi speaks (in the film's French DVD audio commentary) of an immense collective joy in the filming of this ecstatic and loving dance sequence, lending anecdotal weight to the spectator's intuition that the scene truly works as the irremediably cynical film's sole moment of real grace. But how can the dance perform a cohesive or bonding function in the mind of the spectator, scarred as she or he inevitably is by the memories of what will happen to this dancing couple, of the sexual violence they will know? Assaulted on both sides of the dance – psychologically by the early scene of post-divorce rape, and musically by the subsequent plunge into Whigfield's terrifyingly alienating hit 'Saturday Night' – the spectator clutches at the loving possibilities of the sequence as at a mocking straw.[9]

9 The lovely ballads of Paolo Conti are used throughout the film to provide (in Ozon's words) 'ironie et distanciation' (French DVD audio commentary). Nowhere is this effect more crushing than at the end of the first sequence, as Marion walks down the hotel corridor after her rape to the beautifully romantic strains of Conti's 'Una Lacrima sul Viso'.

Ozon's plunges into musical territory function, for the most part, then, either as grimly lucid reflections of the power relations already existing within the group, or else as mirages of potential cohesion that will be brutally forced to evaporate. The final category of musical interlude, though, and the one which most properly could be said to perform the 'excessive' aesthetic action I have sought to claim for some of the more arresting moments of Ozonian horror, is the song that penetrates the surface of the film like a wound, filled with a barely containable emotion that threatens to engulf the viewer. In *Gouttes d'eau sur pierres brûlantes*, for example, Franz twice shuts himself in his room to experience music alone. Both times, Franz's own rapturous engagement with the piece of music in question remains unappreciated by the other characters in the flat (first Leopold, then Anna), and his unequivocally intimate relation with the piece confirms still further his outsider status in the performance-obsessed society of the film. Verdi's near-hysterical *Dies Irae*, in the same way as Françoise Hardy's oneiric rendition in German of 'Träume', cannot be choreographed, cannot exist alongside a neatly performed set of dance moves, cannot, the film seems to suggest, be inserted into social relations, which seem to stand as an artificial opposite to the unaffected authenticity of the musical piece in question. During the Verdi piece, Franz, alone and ecstatic, waves his arms in an uncontrolled frenzy, much to the disgust of Leopold; during 'Träume' Ozon's camera spins around the character's head in sympathy with his entrancement, while Anna merely looks on with polite disinterest. The spectator is swept up with the passion of Franz and the pieces themselves, edging ever closer to Franz's inner world. The authentic 'puncture' of the musical experience cannot be recuperated by Franz, however, in his survival and co-existence among the other characters – it is a rapturous supplement that refuses to be integrated. Marie's supermarket stroll in *Sous le sable*, filmed with a dream-like sympathy by Ozon's camera while the French singer Barbara's performance of 'Quel joli temps' plays over the extra-diegetic soundtrack, is infused with exactly the same sense of 'authentic' interiority, sealing the character into a non-performed relation with the music (which, however, appears to be playing only in her head, if at all) that cannot be enjoyed with other characters, only with the equally enraptured spectator. Finally, and in much the same way, Mme Chanel/Firmine Richard's rendition of the Dalida hit 'Pour ne pas vivre seul' in *8 femmes* is notable as the only performance in the entire film which is sung alone, for nobody but the performer herself. With tears pouring from her eyes as she, alone and despised in her kitchen, sings the melancholy paean to the ultimate Ozonian paradigm, the aspiration to 'togetherness' within the sensation of being utterly alone, Richard presents this song as the antithesis to the other women's aggressive weapons of social ascendancy: it is simply an outpouring of wretched sadness, an emotional anomaly that pricks the film's musical landscape of stripteases, posturing and ambiguous calls to unity. That Mme Chanel will, shortly after this performance, 'die' to the rest of the group, entering a catatonic state, and barely uttering another word for the rest of the film, should come as no surprise: her song and its over-stimulated sincerity signals an apparently impossible integration into Ozon's increasingly dominant hegemony of irony and artifice.

Ozonian melodrama: prison, release or pantomime?

Similar tensions exist in Ozon's varying use of a melodramatic aesthetic: at times this too will be employed to prick the surface of the film's texture, therapeutically exploding the worlds of the characters and the senses of the spectator so as to be able to propel them all forward into a new space of sorts. At other times, the melodrama is itself of a stunted, imprisoning, perpetuating strain, merely accentuating the protagonists' multiple entrapments. Analysts of Hollywood film melodrama of the sort exemplified by Douglas Sirk's films of the 1950s have long debated over the question of to what extent the genre can be considered 'progressive'. Where some Marxist critics have suggested that melodrama's almost exclusive concentration on psychological and emotional tensions within the family places too much emphasis on private feeling, thus ignoring wider political contexts and shoring up already-existing patriarchal structures rather than offering alternatives, theorists such as Thomas Elsaesser (1972) and Laura Mulvey (1987) have proposed that, in the hands of the right director, melodrama can serve as a crucial critique, or even a necessarily limited explosion, of repressive social formations. The fact that melodrama operates through such highly emotionally charged aesthetics, narrative and characterisation often creates a certain feeling of hysteria bubbling beneath the surface of the film, an excessive, 'out-of-control', pulsating intensity that threatens to engulf the film and its characters, and take the spectator along with them. The characters themselves may lack self-awareness, may be sealed into psychic and familial traps steeped in conservatism and patriarchy, but the film melodrama's relentless gaze inside those traps, its gaudy, garish emphasis on the characters' fetishist fixations, both material (lavish or excessive décor, dress, etc.) and moral (constant confessions, betrayals, etc.) can end up creating an aesthetic space approaching the feel of a monomaniacal dream. In eschewing the sensible restraint of 'realism', instead forcing the spectator's face into the high-octane frenzy of the family's emotions taken to their deranged zenith, the melodrama might succeed in blowing the supposedly inevitable foundations of modern, post-Freudian forms of kinship and neurosis out of the water.[10] Film melodrama has historically been divided, we might say, then, between: (a) works which are content merely to explore a temporary crisis within the law, ultimately holding back from total explosion, and returning the family back to the spectator in one piece, or at least reconstituted in legally acceptable terms; and (b) works that use their emotional excesses actually to provoke an irrevocable crisis of the very Law that has hitherto glued their characters' worlds together.[11]

Ozon's use of various melodramatic aesthetics shifts between the orchestration of the potentially liberating 'explosions' that sometimes emerge from the genre's very excesses and the sealing-in of character and spectator into melodrama's most rigid familial structures. *Sitcom* and *8 femmes*, for example, both deploy various tropes of classic film melodrama in such a way that, for the majority of the films' duration, entrapment establishes itself as the predominant sensation for both viewer and characters. A feeling of claustrophobia – a typical aspect of the genre – is generated to an almost unbearable point. In *Sitcom*, the

---

10 For an excellently thorough overview of the fascinating critical debates surrounding film melodrama and its ethico-political repercussions see Cook and Bernink, 1999: 157–72.

11 A film melodrama such as Nicholas Ray's *Rebel without a Cause* (1955) might be thus opposed to ones such as Douglas Sirk's *Written on the Wind* (1956): where the former appears to locate its protagonists' subversive activities as arising from the deficiencies of a decadent paternal function that is in urgent need of renewal, the latter goes much further in appearing to locate failure and violence in every vestige of the father-led family unit, a unit which, by the film's end, will prove utterly obsolete.

only spaces outside the family home Ozon allows his puppet-like cast of characters are the office of Hélène's psychoanalyst, the swimming pool of the family counselling centre, and the graveyard of the final sequence. Locations beyond the prison of the family melodrama can only be found, it would seem, in the shape of dubious or dreamlike psychological therapies or in death itself. In *8 femmes*, the characters' numerous attempts to escape the house, to start the car, or even to telephone to the outside world are all doomed to frustration. Incessant talk and chatter – usually analysis of the various trials and tribulations being undergone by the family – so typical of the film melodrama dominate both films, the children of the families proving particularly adept at aping a kind of cod-Freudian discourse around love, sex and neurosis: in *Sitcom* Nicolas and Sophie pontificate in the bath together about their parents' lifeless marriage, while in *8 femmes* Catherine and Suzon discuss the ins and outs of unplanned pregnancy and frigidity. These conversations, however, excessive and abundant though they are, do anything but free the characters from the deadlocks in which they find themselves, melodramatic verbiage proving just another means by which the characters delude themselves that they exercise some kind of control over their environments and psychologies. As for the flashbacks in which both films indulge – another staple ingredient of the film melodrama – these too serve only to mislead, bewilder and further stultify both characters and viewer, leading to anything but insight or progress. For the eight women of *8 femmes*, the various stories they recount to one another about how Papa may or may not have died and about their own (non)involvement are usually false, the images accompanying a given character's mendacious voiceover an additional trap – for the viewer this time – to block movement forward. And when the 'truth' does finally arrive as flashback, in the form of Catherine's climactic explanation, the effect is anything but emotionally cathartic: instead it is a reminder to all involved that the whole day has been a farce orchestrated by Papa himself and daddy's little helper. This is a patriarch no amount of melodramatic interchange or excessive soul-searching can seem to expose or expunge. As for *Sitcom*, Ozon frames its typically melodramatic *in media res* structure – the film begins with the sound of gunshots taking place inside the house before throwing the viewer back three months in time – as a mere red herring. We will eventually realise that the dramatic massacre we have been waiting to see is but a daydream of the father, a puny distraction indeed in comparison with the sheer horror of the rat-metamorphosis denouement that will supplant it in narrative terms.

On a few occasions, Ozon has explored the possibilities of melodramatic forms which, in their very excess, might feasibly be argued to destabilise the terms of the father-dominated framework from which they emerge. In *Gouttes d'eau sur pierres brûlantes* (2000) (a film based on an early play by Fassbinder, who was himself obsessed with the ethical and aesthetic possibilities of Sirkian melodrama and his own German 'anti-melodramas'), the archetypal melodramatic hero Franz seems destined to remain firmly trapped within the nightmarish psycho-sexual prison into which he wanders at the start of the film. The cruel melodrama that is life and love with Leopold is yet another patriarchal labyrinth that appears to offer no chance of emotional transcendence. Franz's endless conversations first with Leopold, then with Anna, and finally with Vera, all seem to seal him more and more tightly into his horrible impasse: trying to express his feelings to Leopold leads merely to anger, punishment and an ever more pitiless insistence by the latter on order and control; with Anna his attempts to find words to pour out his love for Leopold in the frankest, starkest terms possible are met only with disbelief; as for Vera, her bleak, extended reply to his lamentations – the tale of her own ongoing enslavement to Leopold – merely confirms the hopelessness of his situation in depressing and lifeless tones. Melodramatic exchange between characters seems, here, then, once again, no avenue of subversive excess, and Franz's spontaneously seeping, leaking emotion is either brutally clamped down upon or else finds it has no place to go. Where the film *does* start to beat out a new path of sorts via an immersion in melodrama is in its descent, after the definitive arrival of Vera, into an unashamed hyperbolisation of Leopold's power. When all four characters at last find themselves together for the first time, Leopold's status as king of the castle, hitherto always denied, restrained or channelled into hypocritical claims of victimisation, is suddenly magnified in outrageous melodramatic terms: he claps his hands, barks orders at the women to cook, choreographs an improbable obligatory dance, in short, transforms before our very eyes into a caricatural despot, lacking all the subtleties of characterisation that a realist aesthetic, hitherto generally adhered to, would usually demand. As for Anna and Vera, both become – quite improbably – giggling, quaking slave girls, quite suddenly hysterical in their revelry in subjugation. Only Franz remains consistent with the character we have hitherto experienced him to be, unchanged by the film's brusque cartoonish new mode. Melodrama's metamorphosis of the representation of power relations among Leopold, Anna and Vera allows Franz to 'act out' the previously unspoken truth of the situation he is embroiled in: he takes poison and dies. The fabric of the film's *huis clos* dynamic is, at last, punctured, Franz's melodramatic public declaration ('Je suis complètement fou de lui!' – 'I'm totally crazy about him!') and tragicomic suicide allowing both protagonist and spectator a way out at last, and Vera the ineluctable hint that escape may be a good idea for her as well.[12] In the same way, one fruitful way of appreciating Ozon's 2003 film *Swimming Pool* might be to approach it as an experiment in the positive potential – for both character and spectator – of an emotionally overblown, improbable, 'melodramatic' epiphany: Sarah and Julie emerge by the film's climax as contemporary examples of a new kind of women's picture, a Mildred Pierce and Veda in renewed, patriarch-defeating symbiosis rather than self-hating feminine anxiety, enmity and division. Three-quarters of the way through the film – just as was the case in *Gouttes d'eau sur pierres brûlantes* – the hitherto 'realist' contours of the narrative suddenly lurch into *invraisemblance*. From the moment we see Sarah suddenly wake up with a jolt and in a cold sweat after her deep, stoned sleep, only to find Franck missing and Julie inexplicably transformed, it becomes difficult to identify the status of Sarah's – and our – grip on reality. Has the preceding sequence of violence between Franck and Julie merely been a dream concocted by the newly inspired Sarah? Every successive scene pushes Sarah and us further into the realms of hallucinatory murder mystery, excessively revelling in the very trappings of melodrama rather than soberly analysing melodrama's creator – Sarah Morton the crime writer – as it had been content to do up to this point. As Sarah rolls back the swimming pool cover in the nervous anticipation of the discovery of Franck's corpse floating in the water we become suddenly sucked into the non-ironic emotional thrills of suspense. Her subsequent investigations (accompanied by cries such as 'Where did this blood come from?') draw

12 Fiona Handyside (2007a) writes compellingly of *Gouttes d'eau sur pierres brûlantes* and its use of melodrama as profoundly ethical interventions, specifically in the way in which 'Vera and Franz's suffering bodies imply the need for some sort of emotional response from the spectator'.

us more and more deeply into the excesses of flagrant, dreamlike, almost Lynchian emotionalism: Marcel's daughter, we discover, is an ageless dwarf woman, who utters the bewildering declaration that 'La maman de Julie est morte!'; Julie herself enters into a zombie-like state, punctured by hysterical outbursts that are structured by a purely unconscious logic; the flashbacks to Franck's murder itself are filmed in the lurid manner of a low-budget 1950s pulp flick, Julie's naked, bludgeoning form a far cry from the lengthy, tasteful sequences depicting Canderel, plain yoghurt and rustling leaves that had filled the first half of the film. As for the bizarre, and quite unexpected sex scene between Sarah and Marcel the aged gardener, it too intrudes into the film like a strangely fantasised foreign body, its melodramatic function (Sarah is trying to prevent Marcel from mowing the grass and thus discovering Franck's recent burial) intellectually unconvincing yet oddly satisfying at an emotional level. By the time Sarah asks Julie – as the latter is leaving for Saint-Tropez – about her scar, and Julie replies that, so long as the information is for Sarah's book, the origin was a car accident, Ozon's game has become clear: in this new realm all is in the service of tales and fantasies, melodramatic narratives that may be used to produce liberating novels, and to help emotionally 'blocked' characters such as Sarah herself to move forward. That John the publisher is unimpressed by Sarah's finished novel – an unembarrassed and overblown melodrama named *Swimming Pool*, an amalgamation, perhaps, of the Julie-inspired events (both real and fantasised) we have witnessed in the film and the 'stolen' narrative of Julie's mother's unpublished novel – signals the work's excessive nature and its refusal to belong in the cultural space prescribed by the cold lover–father figure who has hitherto controlled Sarah and her work. Their new, melodramatic aesthetic – a potential fusion of three women's lives – will happily go elsewhere.

It seems appropriate to close this survey of Ozon's various excursions into cinematic 'over-stimulation' with a brief consideration of his most excessive film to date, 2006's English-language production *Angel*, based on the 1957 novel by obscure British writer Elizabeth Taylor. Ozon had become interested in making a film of *Angel* some time before he began making *Swimming Pool*: the links between the two films (the inner world of the writer of excessive fiction, the frontiers between realistic and romantic conceptions of existence) are clear, and Ozon states, albeit warning against hasty conclusions, that 'On peut dire que *Swimming Pool* est né de mon envie d'adapter *Angel*' ('You might say that *Swimming Pool* was born from my desire to adapt *Angel*', Rouyer, 2007: 21). For the first time in his career, though, with *Angel* Ozon sets out to make a melodrama through and through, a film that will be the very embodiment of that genre, as well as its implicit critique: rather than simply importing melodramatic elements into an otherwise multidimensional work, Ozon seemingly creates *Angel* for no other reason than to ride at the helm of a veritable melodrama machine. The film is set in Edwardian England, and tells the story of Angel Deverell (played with remarkably unrestrained verve by Romola Garai), a pretty young woman who, despite her working-class background and prosaic relations, is convinced of her brilliance as a writer of romantic fiction. Sure enough, Angel's dreams come true, and she finds herself the literary toast of the nation, publishing successful novel after another, and living in the huge mansion called 'Paradise' in which her sycophantic Aunt Lottie (Janine Duvitski, turning in as painfully comedic a performance as she did as Angela in Mike Leigh's play *Abigail's Party*) had once worked as a servant. The film charts her startling rise to success and her passionate relationship with the stormy painter Esmé (Michael Fassbender), before the unending series of life's disasters begins to set in. Waning popularity, the outbreak of the First World War, Esmé's loss of a leg, infidelity and suicide conspire to leave Angel wretched and destitute, despised by all except the faithful Nora (Lucy Russell), Esmé's plain and adoring sister, who stays with her to her early and grief-stricken death.

In the face of everything – triumphs as well as setbacks – Angel remains, Madame Bovary like, devoted to an essentially imaginary, Romantic vision of the world, where all is saturated with beauty, symbolism and, above all, excess. The conceit at the heart of *Angel* is Ozon's decision to duplicate Angel's absurdly unrealistic vision of existence in every aspect of his manner of filming. Accordingly, the viewer is greeted by an array of colours as vibrant and gaudy as any to be found in *Sitcom* and *8 femmes*: draped by Ozon's regular costume designer Pascaline Chavanne in a selection of deep reds and blushing pinks, Romola Garai as Angel exudes the sweet-smelling artifice of an impossible glamour. (By the time of Angel's downfall, she is still clinging to an improbably drastic wardrobe which, coupled with her drawn and perpetually frenzied expression, makes of her a risible witch figure who terrifies small children.) The opening credits unfold in bright-pink letters against a black background and Philippe Rombï's alternately cutesy and lugubrious score. Scenes of Angel riding in horse and carriage through the streets of London or on honeymoon with Esmé in Egypt are presented in the most laughably synthetic manner possible: the actors are filmed against a blatantly false moving backdrop of Big Ben, the pyramids or some other icon of pseudo-mythical geographies. When Angel, ever-more reminiscent of Scarlett O'Hara, rushes out of 'Paradise' in the pouring rain to propose to Esmé, a huge rainbow emerges behind the two lovers. Ozon insists that this decision to ape Angel's demented sensibility comes not from some witty desire to provide ironic commentary on the protagonist's skewed vision of things, but rather from a sincere desire to enter her world in a spirit of sincere sympathy.[13] The cumulative effect of such a relentless duplication of what amount to being the more vacuous aspects of the melodramatic aesthetic is to render *Angel* not only an utterly alienating cinematic experience, but also a singularly perplexing one. The viewer is excluded from entering Angel's world precisely because Ozon will allow neither protagonist nor film to behave as anything other than vapid and caricatural infants, shrilly spewing one hackneyed commonplace after another, without ever revealing even a hint of the tear-jerking anguish always to be found in the equally overblown, but immeasurably more honest melodramas of Douglas Sirk that Ozon suggests *Angel* is supposed to resemble. Unable to function effectively either as earnest producer of unbridled emotionalism or as devilish deconstruction of that same excessive sensibility, the film ultimately drops in exhaustion before the equally listless viewer, as monstrously swollen with emptiness and self-regard as Angel herself. This could, of course, in many ways be held up as Ozon's supreme triumph here: with *Angel* Ozon creates a beautiful folly every bit as deranged, insubstantial and deeply unfashionable as the heroine herself. As Esmé tells Angel, with a great deal of insight, the singular thing about her writing is that it seems to operate as a dialogue with itself, text written purely with the author's own stimulation in mind, not that of her readers, whose potential pleasure, edifi-

---

13 'Je n'ai pas hésité à pousser à l'extrême l'utilisation de certains clichés. Pour moi, il n'y a là aucune ironie. C'est très premier degré, juste pour entrer dans son monde' ('I didn't hesitate to push my use of certain clichés to extremes. There was no irony for me in that. It's very sincere, just as a way to enter her world') (Rouyer, 2007: 24).

cation or transformation exist merely as quite optional supplements. Ozon's numerous cinematic experiments with various forms of over-stimulation may well, despite one's best efforts to ascribe to them a somehow 'useful' function, turn out to function in precisely the same ecstatically solipsistic fashion.

References

Cook, Pam and Bernink, Mieke (eds) (1999) *The Cinema Book*, London, British Film Institute.

Creed, Barbara (1993) *The Monstrous-Feminine: Film, Feminism, Psychoanalysis*, London, Routledge.

Elsaesser, Thomas (1972) 'Tales of sound and fury: observations on the family melodrama', *Monogram* 4: 2–15.

Gaitandis, Anastasios and Curk, Polona (2007) *Narcissism: A Critical Reader*, London, Karnac.

Hain, Mark (2007) 'Explicit ambiguity: sexual identity, Hitchcockian criticism, and the films of François Ozon', *Quarterly Review of Film and Video*, 24(3): 277–88.

Handyside, Fiona (2007) 'Melodrama and ethics in François Ozon's *Gouttes d'eau sur pierres brûlantes*', *Studies in French Cinema*, 7: 3.

Mulvey, Laura (1987) 'Notes on Sirk and melodrama', in C. Gledhill (ed.), *Home is Where the Heart Is: Studies in Melodrama and the Women's Film*, London, British Film Institute, 75–82.

Rouyer, Philippe (2007) 'L'ironie et l'émotion', *Positif*, 553: 21–5.

Plantinga, C. and Smith, G. M. (eds) (1999) *Passionate Views: Films, Cognition and Emotion*, Baltimore/London, John Hopkins University Press.

Shaviro, Steven (1993) *The Cinematic Body*, Minneapolis/London, University of Minnesota Press.

Williams, Linda (1995) 'Film bodies: gender, genre and excess', in B. K. Grant (ed.), *Film Genre Reader II*, Austin, University of Texas Press.

Žižek, Slavoj (2000) *The Art of the Ridiculous Sublime: On David Lynch's Lost Highway*, Washington, University of Washington Press.

Zupančič, Alenka (2000) *Ethics of the Real*, London/New York, Verso.

Internet sources

www.francois-ozon.com, accessed July 2007.

A drop in the ocean: concluding remarks

With *Angel*, released in France in March 2007, François Ozon's cinema has clearly shifted in a new direction, the exact nature and implications of which it is hard to pinpoint. As Ozon himself put it in an interview with French film journal *Positif*, 'Il est vrai qu'avec ce film j'ai eu le sentiment d'être allé au bout de quelque chose. Je ne saurais pas trop dire quoi, mais j'ai senti qu'il fallait un profond renouvellement, partir sur de nouvelles bases' ('It's true that with this film I've got the feeling of having gone to the end of something. I wouldn't be able to say what exactly, but I felt the need for a profound renewal, to set off from new foundations'). Asked what direction he now intends to pursue, he replies, with a certain wariness: 'D'habitude, je pars tout de suite sur autre chose. Mais, pour la première fois, j'ai un peu de mal' ('Normally, I set off straight away on something else. But, for the first time, I'm having a bit of trouble', Rouyer, 2007: 25.) How might we try to express the character of Ozon's cinema before this putative watermark?

The eight feature films written for the screen and directed by Ozon between 1998 and 2005, as well as the numerous shorts he made in the decade before *Sitcom*, may be regarded as an astonishingly coherent set of cinematic essays on the radical transformation of human life, treated in a variety of different ways, ranging quite literally from the sublime to the ridiculous. Whether the prey of a magical rat or a mysterious ogre, as in the early features, or struggling with the various deaths and desertions that have dogged Ozon's cinema since *Sous le sable*, Ozon's protagonists between *Victor* and *Le Temps qui reste* are confronted with sudden and violent catalysts for metamorphosis. The transformations that these protagonists undergo are always reflected by equally dramatic lurches in the aesthetics of the film itself. The spectator, like the characters themselves, crosses a Rubicon from which no return is possible. These crossings may be provoked by Ozon's troubling experiments with genre, as explored in the previous chapter, or they may come about quite simply in narrative terms, as we share the protagonists' dramatic voyages between dimensions and realms. With *Swimming Pool*'s Sarah Morton, we journey quite suddenly from the grey skies of the Thames to the blinding light of the south of France; with *5x2*'s Marion and Gilles, we leap (in time as well as space) from the gloomy interiors of a Paris lawyer's offices to the sparkling waters of summery Italy. If *Angel* emerges as such a strangely 'un-Ozonian' film – although it may well come to be the blueprint for an entirely new kind of Ozon film – this surely has as much to do with its uniformity of tone, geography and characterisation as with its English-speaking cast and uncharacteristically long running time. For neither Angel nor *Angel* actually go anywhere. As overblown at their beginnings as they are at their endings, both exist throughout at the same fever pitch, literally refusing to move, remaining stubbornly faithful to a whimsical vision they have conceived independently of contact with anyone or anything related to lived experience, and from which nothing will shake them. The Ozon cycle from 1993 to 2005, on the other hand, explores events and situations that (sometimes literally) blow their protagonists to smithereens, prodding them towards reassemblage in radically new environs, pulling them in and out of familiar and deeply unfamiliar frames, experimenting constantly with the all-pervasive prodding of change. Ozon's cinema prior to *Angel* has, above all, been a cinema concerned with the recording of the metamorphoses wrought in human life by the intervention of forces beyond human control. His camera is often keener, in films like *Swimimng Pool* or *5x2*, to capture a character's rapt sensation at feeling the sun on her face or the wind in her hair than it is in representing that same character's response to another human being. The intrusion of otherworldly, fantastical entities has a far greater impact on early Ozonian protagonists than the tedious machinations of their families and friends. And, combining the spirit of both nature and the supernatural in its cosmic effect on the human lives it dwarfs, the ocean, together with the beach it noisily laps, return, in Ozon's cinema, with an insistence that is impossible to ignore. 'La plage, chez Ozon, c'est toujours le lieu où la bourgeoisie en vacances se frotte avec ce qui l'excède, où son goût pour la nature sauvage l'entraîne au-delà de ce qu'elle pouvait imaginer' ('The beach, in Ozon, is always the place where the middle classes on holiday rub up against what is greater than they are, where their taste for wild nature drags them beyond their wildest dreams', Blouin, 2001: 76). Devoted to the aural, visual and narrative exploration of this unstoppable location of otherness, Ozon's cinema truly does see the sea, and commands that it be seen, carving out a cinematic space in calm thrall to the enormity in which characters such as Sasha, Marie, Marion and Romain are so often swallowed up.

François Ozon's first two decades of filmmaking have offered audiences contact with one of the most dynamic forces to have emerged out of French cinema in the post-New Wave period. Ozon has consistently played with the stakes of what may be signified by 'transgression' in the cinema, his films showing again and again that, while clearly intrigued by (and well aware of the spectatorial appeal of) an ongoing experimentation with the on-screen representation of surprising forms of sexuality and violence, the areas of human existence most in need of filmic exploration are precisely those which elude naming altogether, dimensions of experience both cosmic and spectral. While on the surface far more light-hearted and fashion conscious than directors such as Bergman, Bresson or Ozu – all filmmakers more obviously associated with a spiritual or mystical sensibility – Ozon has in fact demonstrated a comparable commitment to their singularity of post-earthly vision, a singularity that is sometimes as perplexing as it is clearly out of vogue. Whether that singularity develops the potential for a genuinely transformational vision of the world, subjectivity and human relations, or whether it continues its drift towards the eccentricities of a self-pleasuring and ironical cinematic baroque, only time will tell.

References

Blouin, Patrice (2001) 'La place du mort', *Cahiers du cinéma*, 554: 76–8.
Rouyer, Philippe (2007) 'L'ironie et l'émotion', *Positif*, 553: 21–5.

Filmography

1986–1992: Several short films on video and Super 8, including: *Les Doigts dans le ventre* (1988), *Photo de famille* (1988), *Mes parents un jour d'été* (1990), *Une Goutte de sang, Peau contre peau (les risques inutiles), Le Trou madame, Deux plus un* (all 1991) and *Thomas reconstitué* (1992).

Victor (1993) 14 mins, 35mm, col.

Director: François Ozon
Screenplay: François Ozon, Nicolas Mercier
Cinematographer: Sylvia Calle
Sound: Benoît Hillebrant
Editor: Thierry Bordes
Cast: François Genty, Isabelle Journeau, Jean-Jacques Forbin, Laurent Labasse, Martine Erhel
Production: Femis

Une Rose Entre Nous (1994) 27 mins, 35mm, col.

Director: François Ozon
Screenplay: François Ozon, Nicolas Mercier
Cinematographer: Sylvia Calle
Sound: Benoît Hillebrant
Editor: Sylvie Ballyot
Cast: Sasha Hails, Rodolphe Lesage, Christophe Hemon, Jacques Disses, Francis Arnaud, Gilles Frilay
Production: Femis

Action Vérité (1994) 4 mins, 35mm, col.

Screenplay, editor and director: François Ozon
Cinematographer: Yorick Le Saux
Sound: Benoît Hillebrant
Cast: Fabien Billet, Adrien Pastor, Farida Rahmatoullah, Aylin Argun
Production: Fidélité Productions

Jospin s'éclaire (documentary, 1995) 52 mins, col.

La Petite Mort (1995) 26 mins, 35mm, col.

Director: François Ozon
Screenplay: François Ozon, Didier Blasco
Cinematographer: Yorick Le Saux
Editor: Frédéric Massiot
Designer: Juliette Cheneau
Cast: François Delaive, Camille Japy, Martial Jacques, Michel Beaujard
Production: Fidélité Productions

Une Robe d'été (1996) 15 mins, 35mm, col.

Screenplay and director: François Ozon
Cinematographer: Yorick Le Saux
Sound: Benoît Hillebrant
Editor: Jeanne Moutard
Cast: Frédéric Mangenot, Lucia Sanchez, Sébastien Charles
Production: Fidélité Productions
Song 'Bang Bang' sung by Sheila

Scènes de Lit (1997) 26 mins, 35mm, col.

Screenplay and director: François Ozon
Cinematographers: Yorick Le Saux, Matthieu Vadepied
Cast: Valérie Druguet, Camille Japy, Lucia Sanchez, François Delaive
Production: Local Films

X2000 (1998) 6 mins, 35mm, col.

Screenplay and director: François Ozon
Cinematographer: Pierre Stroeber
Sound: Benoît Hillebrant
Editor: Dominique Petrot

Cast: Denise Schropfer-Aron, Bruno Slagmulder, Olivier and Lionel Le Guevellou, Lucia Sanchez, Flavien Coupeau
Production: Fidélité Productions and Canal Plus

Regarde la mer (1997) 52 mins, 35mm, col.

Screenplay and director: François Ozon
Cinematographer: Yorick Le Saux
Sound: Daniel Sobrino
Music: Eric Neveux
Cast: Sasha Hails, Marina De Van
Production: Fidélité Productions

Sitcom (1998) 80 mins, 35mm, col.

Screenplay and director: François Ozon
Cinematographer: Yorick Le Saux
Sound: Benoît Hillebrant
Editor: Dominique Petrot
Music: Eric Neveux
Designer: Angélique Puron
Cast: Evelyne Dandry, François Marthouret, Marina et Adrien De Van, Stéphane Rideau, Lucia Sanchez, Jules-Emmanuel Eyoum Deido
Production: Fidélité Productions

Les Amants criminels (1998) 90 mins, 35mm, col.

Screenplay and director: François Ozon
Cinematographer: Pierre Stoeber
Sound: François Guillaume
Editor: Dominique Petrot
Music: Philippe Rombi
Designer: Arnaud de Mauleron
Cast: Natacha Régnier, Jérémie Renier, Miki Manojlovic, Salim Kechiouche, Yasmine Belmadi
Production: Fidélité Productions

Gouttes d'eau sur pierres brûlantes (1999), 90 mins, 35mm, col.

Director: François Ozon
Screenplay: François Ozon, from the stage play written by Fassbinder *Tröpfen auf Heisse Steine*
Cinematographer: Jeanne Lapoirie

Sound: Eric Devulder
Editor: Laurence Bawedin
Designer: Arnaud de Mauleron
Costumes: Pascaline Chavanne
First assistant: Hubert Barbin
Sound mixing: Jean-Pierre Laforce
Music:
'Träume' performed by Françoise Hardy
Symphonie n° 4 en sol majeur (Mahler)
Requiem, 3. 'Dies Irae' (Verdi)
'Zadok the priest' (Handel)
'Tanze Samba Mit Mir' performed by Tony Holiday
Cast: Bernard Giraudeau, Malik Zidi, Anna Thomson, Ludivine Sagnier
Production: Fidélité Productions and Alain Sarde Films

Sous le sable (2000) 95mins, 35mm, col.

Director: François Ozon
Screenplay: François Ozon with Emmanuèle Bernheim, Marina De Van and Marcia Romano
Director of photography: Jeanne Lapoirie, Antoine Heberlé
Sound: Jean-Luc Audy, Benoît Hillebrant, Jean-Pierre Laforce
Casting: Antoinette Boulat
Editor: Laurence Bawedin
Music: Philippe Rombi
Other music:
'Septembre (Quel joli temps)' by Barbara
'Undenied' by Portishead
Prélude Opus 28 en si mineur – Lento assai – by Frédéric Chopin
Prélude en B major – Vivace – by Frédéric Chopin
Symphonie n°2 en Do mineur – Résurrection – by Gustav Mahler
Cast: Charlotte Rampling, Bruno Cremer, Jacques Nolot, Alexandra Stewart, Pierre Vernier, Andrée Tainsy
Production: Olivier Delbosc and Marc Missonnier

8 femmes (2001) 103 mins, 35mm, col.

Director: François Ozon
Screenplay: François Ozon with the collaboration of Marina De Van, adapted from the play by Robert Thomas

Cinematographer: Jeanne Lapoirie
Sound: Pierre Gamet, Jean-Pierre Laforce
Casting: Antoinette Boulat
Editor: Laurence Bawedin
Music: Krishna Lévy
Costumer: Pascalie Chavanne
Art designer: Arnaud de Moléron
Choreographer: Sébastien Charles
Songs:
'Papa t'es plus dans l'coup' by Ludivine Sagnier
'Message Personnel' by Isabelle Huppert
'A quoi sert de vivre libre?' by Fanny Ardant
'Mon Amour, Mon Ami' by Virginie Ledoyen
'Pour ne pas vivre seule' by Firmine Richard
'Pile ou face' by Emmanuelle Béart
'Toi jamais' by Catherine Deneuve
'Il n'y a pas d'amour heureux' by Danielle Darrieux
Cast: Catherine Deneuve, Isabelle Huppert, Emmanuelle Béart, Fanny Ardant, Virginie Ledoyen, Danielle Darrieux, Ludivine Sagnier, Firmine Richard.
Production: Olivier Delbosc and Marc Missonnier (Fidélité Productions)

Swimming Pool (2003) 102 mins, 35mm, col.

Director: François Ozon
Screenplay: François Ozon and Emmanuèle Berheim.
Cinematographer: Yorick Le Saux
Music: Philippe Rombi
Sound: Lucien Balibar
Costumer: Pascaline Chavanne
Make-up: Gill Robillard
Hairdresser: Myriam Roger
Art designer: Wouter Zoon
Editor: Monica Coleman
Sound editor: Benoît Hillebrant, Jean-Pierre Laforce
Cast: Charlotte Rampling, Ludivine Sagnier, Charles Dance, Marc Fayolle, Jean-Marie Lamour, Mireille Mossé, Michel Fau, Jean-Claude Lecas, Lauren Farrow
Production: Olivier Delbosc and Marc Missonnier (Fidélité)

5x2 (2004), 90 mins, 35mm, col.

Director: François Ozon
Screenplay: François Ozon with the collaboration of Emmanuèle Bernheim
Cinematographer: Yorick Le Saux
Sound: Jean-Pierre Duret and Brigitte Taillandier
Cast: Antoinette Boulat ARDA
Assistant director: Hubert Barbin
Editor: Monica Coleman
Sound editor: Jean-Pierre Laforce
Costumer: Pascaline Chavanne
Set photographer: Jean-Claude Moireau
Music: Philippe Rombi
Cast: Valeria Bruni-Tedeschi, Stéphane Freiss, Françoise Fabian, Michael Lonsdale, Antoine Chappey, Géraldine Pailhas, Marc Ruchmann
Production: Olivier Delbosc and Marc Missonnier (Fidélité)

Le Temps qui reste (2005) 90 mins, 35mm, col.

Director: François Ozon
Screenplay: François Ozon
Cinematographer: Jeanne Lapoirie
Editor: Monica Coleman
Cast: Melvil Poupaud, Jeanne Moreau, Valeria Bruni-Tedeschi, Daniel Duval, Marie Rivière, Christian Sengewald, Louise-Anne Hippeau...
Production: Olivier Delbosc and Marc Missonnier (Fidélité)
Music:
Symphonie n°3 composed by Arvo Pärt
Für Alina composed by Arvo Pärt
Tenebrae Factae Sunt composed by Marc-Antoine Charpentier
Postludium composed by Valentin Silvestrov

Un lever de rideau (2006) 30 mins, 35mm, col.

Director: François Ozon
Screenplay: François Ozon, adapted from 'Un incompris' by Henry de Montherlant
Cinematographer: Yorick Le Saux
Editor: Muriel Breton
Art designer: Sébastien Danos

Costumer: Pascaline Chavanne
Sound: Laurent Benaim
Scriptgirl: Annick Reipert
Make-up and hairdresser: Sylvie Longchamp
Set photographer: Jean-Claude Moireau
Sound editor: Benoit Gargonne
Sound mixer: Benjamin Viau
Production manager: Cécile Vacheret
Music: Gonzales
Cast: Louis Garrel, Vahina Giocante, Mathieu Amalric

Angel (2006) 134 mins, 35mm, col.

Director: François Ozon
Screenplay: François Ozon with Martin Crimp, adapted from the novel *Angel* by Elizabeth Taylor
Director of photography: Denis Lenoir
Production designer: Katia Wyszkop
Costumes: Pascaline Chavanne
Editor: Muriel Breton
Sound: Pierre Mertens
Sound editor: Benoît Hillebrant
Assistant Director: Dominique Delany
Make-up: Gill Robillard
Hair: Marese Langan
Music: Philippe Rombi
Cast: Romola Garai, Sam Neill, Lucy Russell, Michael Fassbender, Charlotte Rampling, Jacqueline Tong, Janine Duvitski, Christopher Benjamin, Simon Woods, Jemma Powell
Production: Fidélité Films: Olivier Delbosc and Marc Missonnier

Select bibliography

See also the References section at the end of each chapter.

Essays and articles on Ozon's films

Asibong, Andrew (2005) 'Meat, murder, metamorphosis: the transformational ethics of François Ozon', *French Studies*, 59(2): 203–15.

— (2008), 'Spectres of substance: François Ozon and the aesthetics of embodied haunting', in K. Griffiths and D. Evans (eds), *Haunting Presences: Ghosts in French Literature, Theory, Film and Photography*, Cardiff, University of Wales Press.

Bingham, Adam (2003) 'Identity and love: the not-so discreet charm of François Ozon', *Kinoeye*, 3(13), www.kinoeye.org/03/13/bingham13. php, accessed July 2007.

Blouin, Patrice (2001) 'La place du mort', *Cahiers du cinéma*, 554: 76–8.

Chilcoat, Michelle (2005) 'Queering the family in François Ozon's *Sitcom*', in R. Griffiths (ed.), *Queer Cinema in Europe*, Bristol, Intellect Books.

Diamond, Diana (2007) 'Loss, mourning and desire in midlife: François Ozon's *Under the Sand* and *Swimming Pool*', in A. Sabbadini (ed.), *Projected Shadows: Psychoanalytic Reflections on the Representation of Loss in European Cinema*, London, Routledge.

Enjolras, Laurence (2007) 'Etale visuelle, ressac textuel: *Regarde la mer* de François Ozon', *Contemporary French and Francophone Studies*, 11(1): 47–57.

Frankiel, Rita V., '*Sous le sable [Under the Sand]* (2001)' *International*

Journal of Psychoanalysis, 83(1): 313–17.

Hain, Mark (2007) 'Explicit ambiguity: sexual identity, Hitchcockian criticism, and the films of François Ozon', *Quarterly Review of Film and Video*, 24(3): 277–88.

Handyside, Fiona (2007a) 'Melodrama and ethics in François Ozon's *Gouttes* d'eau sur pierres brûlantes', *Studies in French Cinema*, 7:3.

(2007b) 'alternative inheritances: rethinking what adaptation might mean in François Ozon's *Le Temps qui reste* (2005)', *Literature Film Quarterly*, forthcoming.

Ince, Kate (2008) 'François Ozon', in K. Ince (ed.), *Auteurship from Assayas to Ozon: Five Directors*, Manchester, Manchester University Press.

Jousse, Thierry (1997) 'Sans toit ni loï', *Cahiers du cinéma*, 519: 66–7.

Lalanne, Jean-Marc Lalanne (1998) 'La Place du père et celle du rat', *Cahiers du cinéma*, 524: 107–8.

— (2002) 'Les Actrices', *Cahiers du cinéma*, 565: 82–3.

Marvier, Marie (2003) Interview with François Ozon about *Swimming Pool*, *Synopsis*, 25: 14–21.

Rouyer, Philippe (2007) 'L'ironie et l'émotion', *Positif*, 553: 21–5.

Schiller, Britt-Marie, 'On the threshold of the creative imagination: *Swimming* Pool (2003)' *International Journal of Psychoanalysis*, 86:557–66.

Schilt, Thibaut, 'François Ozon', www.sensesofcinema.com/contents/directors/04/ozon.html, accessed July 2007.

Spoiden, Stéphane (2002) 'No man's land: genres en question dans *Sitcom*, *Romance* et *Baise-moi*', *L'Esprit Créateur*, 42(1): 96–106.

Writing and interviews by Ozon

Ozon, Francois (2002) *8 Femmes*, Paris, Editions de la Martinière.

Various documents on the official Ozon website, www.francois-ozon.com

The commentaries by Ozon and many of the crucial figures who work with him (actors, set designers, co-writers, costume designers) on the French DVDs of his films are extremely useful.

Index

Note: 'n.' after a page reference indicates the number of a note on that page. All references in italics are to films, unless otherwise indicated.